Gertrud von le Fort

Gertrud von le Fort

An Introduction
to the Prose Work

Ita O'Boyle

FORDHAM UNIVERSITY PRESS

1964

Contents

Author's Note

THE PAGE REFERENCES to von le Fort's work throughout this *Introduction* refer to the collected edition of her prose fiction, *Erzählende Schriften* (in three volumes), published by Ehrenwirth Verlag, München/Insel Verlag, Wiesbaden, 1956. This is abbreviated throughout as *Schriften*.

The English translations throughout, from von le Fort's work, are in all cases those of the author.

The author wishes to thank the editor of *German Life and Letters* for permission to reproduce here some material from her article "Die Letzte am Schafott," published in that journal in January, 1962.

I.O'B.

Introduction

GERMAN WRITING today may be divided into two broad streams. One of these, comprised of young men and women who started to write in the years after World War II, may be regarded as the literary avant garde; the second stream is made up of writers of the generation who were already well known before the war. Of these two groups the younger writers are more numerous and attract wider publicity. Collectively known as Group 47, they have the common aim of renewing German writing and bringing it into line with the latest literary developments in Europe, of bridging the gap caused by the Nazi censorship, the war and its aftermath. Their work is characterized by a note of critical cynicism: they dissect and analyze their country's weaknesses and failures with a perceptive eye and give expression to their observations in terms of mordant satire. As a target they frequently take such subjects as the less pleasant aspects of Germany's economic miracle, the bribery and corruption in high places and the sheeplike and hypocritical attitude of the mass of the people, whom they see as being only too ready to forget the recent past and to push below the margin of consciousness their feelings of cumulative guilt. Typical of this new generation of writers is Günter Grass, whose novel, *The Tin Drum*, has been the biggest literary sensation of recent years in Germany. While from a literary and stylistic point of view the work of Group 47 is exciting and stimulating, on another level it is deeply disturbing to the Christian reader. The novels of many of these young and talented writers are informed by a complete nihilism and by a contempt for their Christian heritage. They are the inheritors and the perpetuators of Nietzsche's godless world, and their clever and sarcastic indictments of contemporary society spring from a profound scepticism about the purpose of man's life and his ultimate destiny.

The older generation of writers who go to make up the second stream stand in marked contrast to the members of Group 47. They are not concerned to make a break with literary traditions or to develop new methods of exploring human consciousness but, on the contrary, show a deep respect for their literary and cultural heritage. Gertrud von le Fort, who first became widely known in the early 1930's, but whose popularity and appeal have increased enormously in the course of the past decade, belongs to this older generation. Like the younger writers, le Fort is acutely and painfully aware of the sickness of modern society; where she differs from them is in her determination to discover the cause of this sickness and to point to a positive remedy for it. As a convert to Catholicism le Fort's world is theocentric, and she is, accordingly, often dismissed by many of the avant garde as old-fashioned and limited. To the Christian reader, however, tired of the depressingly large number of modern novels that tell repeatedly of the hopeless struggle of man in a universe devoid of meaning, her work offers a sane and balanced assessment of contemporary problems and a positive assertion of the Christian way of life in literary terms.

Gertrud von le Fort is a writer who is engagée. She has committed herself wholly to an ideal, and this ideal finds expression in her work. She is concerned with the human predicament at a fundamental level and is convinced that order, peace and justice can prevail in Western Europe only if it will revert to those Christian values it has abandoned, and for which it has as yet found no substitute. The intensity and urgency with which le Fort presents her themes represent her effort to convey to the reader her own positive view of life seen in its relation to the Creator. She is possessed to a high degree of that quality of compassion so essential to the artist, a compassion which, placed in the context of le Fort's particular background, seems to amount to a sense of responsibility for her age. Whereas it would be an exaggeration to assert that a rationalized sense of mission informs her creative activity, it is nonetheless true that, as she seeks to give literary expression to her deeply-felt convictions about the relevance of Christianity to everyday living, she, like François Mauriac, could assert: "Being a Christian, my Christian beliefs dominate my novels, not because I want to make propaganda for Christianity, but because it is the deepest part of my nature. . . I am a Christian first and last, which means a man responsible to God and to his conscience for the epoch he lives in. . . he has been put here to play a certain role among his fellowmen. He *is* engaged: it isn't a question of deliberately engaging himself."[1] Le Fort's literary work is consistently informed by her personal ideological commitment and the theme of responsibility on various levels is, accordingly, one which finds a prominent place in her writing. We shall see later how it is worked out in some of her novels and short stories.

Our understanding and appreciation of le Fort's work are deepened if we relate it to her background and upbringing. Most of the biographical information available about her comes from a short article entitled *Mein Elternhaus*[2] (My Home). The family, as the name indicates, is of French origin. Her father's ancestors were Huguenots who, rather than renounce their faith in times of persecution, fled from Savoy and found refuge with Calvin in Geneva in the sixteenth century. They migrated from Switzerland to Russia and eventually settled in Germany in the eighteenth century.

Although le Fort's father, a titled army officer, was not a practicing member of any particular religious sect, he nonetheless had a profound respect for the beliefs of others; to him "the great heroic tradition of our family was primarily the absolute obligation to cleave to one's convictions";[3] in her subsequent conversion to Catholicism Gertrud von le Fort carried on this tradition. During her early formative years she was much influenced by her father, who was

> not merely interested in history, but also in philosophy. . . . That philosophy which appealed most to him was the Kantian philosophy. He believed in a moral world order which he saw manifested not only in the life of individuals but in the general movements of history—the categorical imperative was for him a vital directive. In my early years this approach was a formative influence in arriving at moral standards which I have never abandoned.[4]

While the philosophic outlook of Freiherr von le Fort impressed his daughter, of equal importance for her literary work was the interest in history he communicated to her. He emphasized to the young Gertrud that the family were barons of the old German Empire and "he felt part and parcel of German history in its totality and its membership of the European community. Through this attitude of mind he opened to me historical perspectives which remained indelibly impressed on my mind."[5] This inherited interest in history informs very many of le Fort's works and explains her facility in reproducing so accurately the historical background of her fiction. Moreover, she never views an historical event as an isolated incident but—as will be particularly clear in the case of *The Wedding at Madgeburg*—always endeavors to show its deeper significance in the context of world history.

The influence of le Fort's mother on her subsequent development was different from that of her father, but was no less important. The favorite reading of her mother, who was deeply religious, was the Bible and the hymns of Paul Gerhardt. She transmitted to her daughter her "deep appreciation of poetry,"[6] as well as her faith in Christ as the visible proof of God's love for man. Gertud von le Fort still regards her own faith in the love and mercy of Christ—a faith first awakened by her mother—as the factor which, even after her conversion, still binds her to the traditions of her family: "My allegiance to this faith constitutes the basic line of my religious life; it forms the indissoluble link with the Christian spirit prevailing in my parents' home and with the profoundly religious tradition of my family."[7]

The interest in philosophy, history and religion which formed such an important part of the intellectual background of her parents' home was maintained by Gertud von le Fort, and when she went to Heidelberg to pursue her studies the subjects she chose were history and theology. There her enthusiasm was further stimulated by the eminent Protestant theologian, Professor Ernst Troeltsch, one of whose main concerns was the inter-relation of religion and culture. When Troeltsch was subsequently called to a chair at the University of Berlin, le Fort went there to continue her studies. The fact that she was responsible for the posthumous edition of his *Glaubenslehre* in 1923 indicates his deep influence on her thought. To what extent a dissatisfaction with Troeltsch's teaching prompted le Fort to seek a secure spiritual home in the Catholic faith is a question which has given rise to much speculation among critics of her work. It is certainly true that Troeltsch unwittingly played a role in leading le Fort to Catholicism, as she herself has recorded:

> Troeltsch exercised a profound influence on me although I never completely accepted his liberal theories, for I belonged to a family who were adherents of a positive religious faith. But the richness and profundity of his mind opened up for me the world of theological thought, the world of Christian mysticism—and, moreover, the world of religious problems. From his premises I could not arrive at ultimate scientific conclusions, but his deeply religious nature forced me to arrive at a personal solution. Consequently I have always regarded him as having helped to determine the subsequent course of my life.[8]

Other than this le Fort has given no precise reasons for her conversion; she has, however, indicated to the author that it is mistaken to attribute it to any one factor alone. It is not the concern of the literary critic to intrude on her privacy in this respect: to him the only relevant questions are whether the convert has succeeded in fusing the new religious experience with her previous outlook to comprise a new and real unity, and what effect it has had on her writing. It is clear that with regard to le Fort we may speak of such a fusion as having taken place; let us now briefly outline the importance of her conversion for her literary work.

We are lucky in having in le Fort's own words an account of her first contact with the world of Catholic thought. This occurred when, in the early years after the end of World War I, she by chance came across a copy of the periodical *Hochland*, edited by the Jesuit, Karl Muth. Immediately attracted by the note of hope it struck in the general disillusionment of the aftermath of the war, she felt a certain spiritual and intellectual affinity with the ideas expressed in its pages:

This journal in its whole tone seemed to embrace my most treasured possessions, everything that I had inherited from my pious Protestant home. This impression of an all-embracing attitude was the veritable essence of this unforgetable encounter. For the first time in my life I became fully and consciously aware that, notwithstanding all the unhappy tensions and divisions within Christianity, there exists a common heritage of Christian culture. . . in other words I came into contact with the real essence of Catholicism.[9]

From these words it is clear that le Fort's dominant impression as a result of this first contact with the world of Catholic culture was a consciousness of its comprehensive nature;[10] the importance of this experience lies in the fact that it proved to be an accurate foreshadowing of a similar experience on the religious level some years later when she entered the Catholic Church. Let us turn to her own words again for an account of what this contact meant for her:

For the outsider the decisive factor in his first encounter with the Church is that great awareness of her all-embracing maternal attitude. The convert is not someone who expressly stresses the painful nature of his relinquishing of his past beliefs. His essential experience is not that of going over to another faith but an overwhelming awareness of the unity of faith.[11]

These words make it quite clear that le Fort's own experience as a convert has impressed on her very strongly the importance of emphasizing the essential unity of Christendom and of stressing those aspects of belief which unite Christians of different denominations. These convictions are basic to her thought and find repeated expression in her work.

Apart from its function in determining so many of her basic ideas, le Fort's conversion to Catholicism is important to the literary critic since it proved to be the starting point of her career as a novelist. For many years critics have been puzzled by the fact that her literary talents should have come to such late fruition; she was born in 1876, yet before 1924, when her *Hymnen an die Kirche* (Hymns to the Church) were published, no works of fiction appeared under her name. She did, however, publish some short stories and poems under a nom-de-plume, but these were not widely circulated. It seems reasonable to assume that these juvenilia, which she refuses to re-issue today, were of an essentially ephemeral nature, and that they are not important for her subsequent literary work. For our purposes le Fort's creative activity as a novelist began in 1928 with the publication of *The Roman Fountain*. The question immediately presents itself: to what factors may such an abundant late flowering of her poetic talent be attributed? The key to the answer to this question would seem to lie in her conversion, which was clearly the result of a spiritual experience of great depth and intensity. Le Fort's literary work may be looked on as an expression of the fusion of the elements of her family tradition outlined above with experiences of her later life which had their origin in her conversion.

Le Fort the convert sees the contemporary world in a new light. She perceives that modern Europeans have lost that awareness of the supernatural which was the hallmark of preceding centuries. To this loss of traditional belief she ascribes the loss of an ethical center to man's life and also the contemporary spirit of unease and the characteristic malaise of our time. The problems of our age in all their manifold manifestations are of paramount importance for her, and her active mind is constantly concerned to find a satisfying solution to them. In her prose work she gives cogent and succinct expression to this preoccupation.

The problems treated by le Fort are vital issues for the

present age. Since her first novel appeared in 1928 she has experienced the rise of Nazism, the horrors of the 1939-45 war, the defeat and subsequent recovery of her country. The effect which these various experiences have had on her is reflected in her fiction, where they and their concomitant problems have found literary expression. The problem of evil, together with the means of overcoming it, occurs persistently, as does that of the basic insecurity of man in the modern world. Le Fort's approach to these questions is never defeatist or pessimistic. Despite the nature of all she has witnessed, her belief in the divine ordinance of human life and in her basic tenets has remained unshaken. Her fiction offers the reader a constructive approach to the study of the human predicament and her whole output is permeated by her affirmative *Weltanschauung*.

While the themes are basically determined by her beliefs and convictions, the method in which these are presented is also determined by a factor connected with le Fort's background, namely, her interest in history. Very many of the novels and short stories are set in an historical context, and the penetration and exactitude with which she pinpoints the parallel between the historical and the contemporary situation are evidence of her deep understanding of the movements of history. They are not simply to be designated historical novels, colorful and vivid evocations of bygone days, or to be dismissed as a means of escape from the disquieting problems of the present. Indeed le Fort has expressly indicated that she does not regard the historical setting "as an escape from our own age, but as a vantage point from which to arrive at a more rigorous appraisal of our own age and time."[12] Her immediate starting point is always a contemporary situation and it is in order to view this in a more detached and clear perspective that she sets so much of her work against an historical background.

Despite the fact that Gertrud von le Fort celebrated her eighty-fifth birthday a few years ago, her prolific literary activity is as yet continuing and since the war she has published a series of essays on a wide variety of topics, a collection of poems, a volume of autobiographical reminiscences and a very large number of short stories. The many honors and distinctions conferred on her in recent years bear witness to her increasing popularity in her native country. She was awarded the *Gottfried Keller Prize*, one of the major literary awards, in 1952, was given an honorary doctorate by the University of Munich in 1956 and was invited to write the opening hymn for the Eucharistic Congress in Munich in 1960. The numerous translations of her works indicate that she is also becoming well known abroad. The time now seems ripe to introduce English-speaking readers to her work, and this book is intended as an introduction to some of le Fort's novels and short stories for readers who may not be already familiar with her fiction.

A variety of factors have determined the selection of books chosen for examination here. *The Wreath of Angels* and *The Wedding at Magdeburg* have been selected because it seemed desirable to select for detailed study some novels which are characteristic both of her thought and her manner of expression: by also including a discussion of her first novel, *The Roman Fountain*, it is hoped that the reader will get some picture of the development that has taken place in her literary technique. *The Song at the Scaffold*, le Fort's best known work, seemed an obvious choice for an *Introduction*, and *Gate of Heaven* was selected from among her more recent short stories as it is indicative of the way her thought has kept pace with modern developments. Such a selection inevitably means that her earlier work is better represented than her more recent work but this in itself is perhaps not a disadvantage. In assessing the very recent productions of any writer the critic is in the unhappy position of being too close to them in time to see them in proper perspective and is faced with many difficulties in objectively assessing and appraising their true value. It might also be mentioned at this point that le Fort's range of themes is not extensive and that her more recent stories, though original in form and treatment, for the most part re-echo the themes of the earlier works discussed here. *The Tower of Constancy* (*Der Turm der Beständigkeit*), a variation in miniature on the theme of *The Wedding at Magdeburg*, is a case in point. The following selection of her works has been made chiefly on the basis that among them they give a fair picture of le Fort as a writer both of novels and novellen; they cover the most representative aspects of her thought and her method of presenting her basic themes.

To the author, le Fort seems less important and interesting as a stylistic innovator than as an exponent of ideas. A detailed analysis of her work from a stylistic view point is therefore not envisaged here,[13] though it is hoped that the following discussion of her work will show both her strength and weakness as a literary figure and give a fair measure of her versatility as an artist. The primary concern of this *Introduction* is, however, to examine the recurrent themes in the prose work of an author who offers through her fiction a sound and positive approach to important issues of our time.

INTRODUCTION

1. François Mauriac in an interview with Philip Toynbee. *The Observer*, October 27, 1957.
2. *Aufzeichnungen und Erinnerungen* (Benziger, 1951), pp. 11-26.
3. Die grosse heroische Tradition der Familie bedeutete in erster Linie die unbedingte Pflicht, zu seiner Überzeugung zu stehen. *Ibid.*, pp. 22, 23.

4. Nicht nur eine historisch gestimmte, sondern auch eine philosophische Natur. . . Die Philosophie, die seinem Charakter am meisten entsprach, war die Philosophie Kants. Er glaubte an eine sittliche Weltordnung, die er im Leben des einzelnen, aber auch im allgemeinen geschichtlichen Geschehen wirksam sah— der kategorische Imperatif war für ihn ein schöpferischer Befehl. Auch in dieser Richtung liegen für mich früh gebildete, unverlierbare Massstäbe. *Ibid.*, pp. 21, 22.

5. Sondern er bekannte sich zum Ganzen der deutschen Geschichte und zu deren Zusammenhang mit der europäischen. Gerade in dieser Hinsicht öffnete er mir historische Horizonte, die. . . nie wieder verloren gehen konnten. *Ibid.*, p. 15.

6. Ausgesprochener Sinn für Poesie. *Ibid.*, p. 24.

7. Im Glauben an ihn. . . liegt die einheitliche Linie meines eigenen religiösen Lebens. . . es liegt darinnen die unlösbare Verbindung mit dem christlichen Geiste meines Elternhauses und der grossen religiös betonten Tradition meiner Familie. *Ibid.*, p. 25.

8. Troeltsch hat mich sehr tief beeinflusst, ohne dass ich mir seine liberale Theorie ganz zu eigen machte, denn ich stammte aus einem positivgläubigen Elternhause. Aber der Reichtum und der Ernst seines Geistes erschlossen mir die Welt des theologischen Denkens überhaupt, die Welt der christlichen Mystik und der christlichen Philosophie und Ethik-allerdings auch die Welt der religiösen Problematik. Troeltsch konnte von seinen Voraussetzungen her eine letzte wissenschaftliche Entscheidung nicht treffen, aber seine tiefe Religiösität stellte uns auf die persönliche Entscheidung. Von daher habe ich meinen eigenen späteren Weg doch immer als von ihm mitvorbereitet angesehen. Letter quoted by K. H. Groensmit, in *Gertrud von le Fort* (Nijmegen, 1950), p. 1.

9. Weil die ganze Haltung dieser Zeitschrift meine teuersten Besitztümer, das Erbe meines frommen, protestantischen Elternhauses, gleichsam mit einzuschliessen schien. Ja gerade dieser Eindruck des Einschliessenden war das eigentliche Wesen dieser unvergesslichen Begegnung! Ich erlebte damals zum erstenmal mit vollem Bewusstsein, dass es trotz aller schmerzlichen Spannungen und Spaltungen innerhalb des Christentums den gemeinsamen Besitz einer christlichen Kultur gibt. . . ich erlebte also damals das Wesen des wahrhaft Katholischen überhaupt. "Zum 70 Geburtstag von Karl Muth," *Aufzeichnungen*, p. 78.

10. This experience of le Fort's recalls that of another famous convert, Msgr. Ronald Knox, who has described his conversion as his "spiritual Aeneid" and has written: "An Aeneid involves not merely coming home, but coming home to a place you have

never been before, one that combines in itself all that you valued in the old home with added promises of a future that is new." *A Spiritual Aeneid* (London, 1918), p 1.

11. Das Entscheidende in der Begegnung mit der Kirche ist doch für den von aussen Kommenden auch wiederum jenes grosse Innewerden einer einschliessenden mütterlich umfangenden Gebärde. Der Konvertit. . . ist nicht ein Mensch, welcher die schmerzliche konfessionelle Trennung ausdrücklich betont, sondern im Gegenteil einer, der sie überwunden hat: sein eigentliches Erlebnis ist nicht das eines anderen Glaubens, zu dem er "übertritt," sondern sein Erlebnis ist das der Einheit des Glaubens, die ihn überflutet. "Zum 70. Geburtstag von Karl Muth," *Aufzeichnungen,* p. 79.

12. Comme une fuite hors de notre temps mais comme le point de départ d'une connaissance plus rigoureuse de notre temps. *La Table Ronde,* November, 1958, p. 64.

13. The reader interested in a more detailed study of her work is referred to the appended Bibliography.

Gertrud von le Fort

CHAPTER I

The Roman Fountain

T wo years after her reception into the Catholic Church in Rome in 1926 Gertrud von le Fort's first novel, *The Veil of Veronica*,[1] subsequently subtitled *The Roman Fountain,* appeared. This novel, which treats of the spiritual development of a young girl and of her conversion to the Catholic faith in Rome, is clearly related to le Fort's personal experience. Its basic theme, that of religious commitment, is one in which le Fort was deeply involved at a personal level at that time, and it is obvious that in writing this book her pen was guided by the first flush of enthusiasm for her new-found spiritual anchorage. Such an enthusiasm on the part of the author accounts for many excellencies of the book, in particular for the involvement the reader feels in its issues; it results also in what appears as one of its main weaknesses, namely, its discursiveness when elaborating the spiritual problems of the characters. While *The Roman Fountain* doubtless contains many autobiographical elements, these are carefully disguised behind fictitious characters and episodes which have no immediately discernible counterparts in reality, and it is idle for the critic to approach the novel with a view to reading a factual basis into the various episodes portrayed.

3

There are three main characters in *The Roman Fountain*: the orphan Veronica, who narrates the story, the grandmother with whom she lives (the latter is given no proper name), and the young German poet, nicknamed Enzio, son of the man the grandmother once loved, who comes to stay as a guest in the household. Rome is the background against which the destiny of each of these three characters is worked out, and the action of the novel springs from their encounter with one another and the interaction of their respective experiences. Rome brings each of them to an appraisal of his metaphysical position and in this many-faceted city all are confronted with a problem of spiritual dimensions. Hence the city of Rome is far more than a vivid and colorful backcloth; it plays an integral part in the development of the characters and, consequently, of the action of the novel. The whole book pulsates with the lifeblood of this city which has the faculty of giving a new dimension and pattern to the lives of its inhabitants. Le Fort presents Rome in its threefold character; the pagan Rome of classical antiquity; the historical Rome, a city of chaos and decay; and Christian Rome, the Eternal City. All three main characters experience Rome under one or other of these aspects, and their relationships with one another and with the city form the structural basis of the novel.

The Roman Fountain is not a novel of action. There are no outward upheavals, no dynamic forces at work against which the characters must struggle. Its theme is unfolded against a smooth-flowing, slow-moving progression of events, yet the term "psychological novel," often used to connote the opposite of the novel of action, does not really indicate the nature of *The Roman Fountain*. Le Fort is more interested in the spiritual than in the psychological implications of the situations she presents, and the reader's attention is directed toward the problems which concern the charac-

4

ters rather than toward their personalities. The particular problems which confront the characters are of paramount importance to le Fort; she considers them to be fundamental to the human condition and independent of any particular social environment. The reader's interest is accordingly focused on these problems, and the social and political background of the day is not important in the development of the action.

From a schematic point of view *The Roman Fountain* resembles Gotthold Lessing's play *Nathan der Weise. Nathan der Weise* is set in Jerusalem, a city on which different civilizations and religions have left their impact, and its action takes place at the time of the Crusades, which have gathered together representatives of various creeds in the Holy Land. Lessing introduces representatives of the three great monotheistic religions, Jewish, Mohammedan and Christian, and links them together in the most tenuous fashion. Similarly, the background of *The Roman Fountain* is Rome—a city which, like Jerusalem, bears the impression of three cultural-religious eras, Apollonian and Dionysian paganism and Christianity. The resemblance between the two works does not end with the similarity of their respective backgrounds but the parallel may be further extended to the characters. As the Jew, Nathan, dominates the scene in Lessing's play, so does the noble figure of the grandmother in le Fort's novel; the position of Recha, brought up without any specific religious education, is analogous to that of Veronica; the simple unquestioning faith, the charity and self-abnegation of the *Klosterbruder* are qualities which characterize the minor figure, Jeanette.

The Roman Fountain is in the long-established tradition of the *Bildungsroman*, the novel of development. This tradition had its origins in the Middle Ages with such works as Wolfram von Eschenbach's *Parzival*, an epic which traced the progress of its hero through the stages of *tumpheit* (state of tutelage) and *zwîfel* (doubt) to *saelde* (happiness and fulfilment). *The Roman Fountain* fits easily into this time-honored pattern and we watch Veronica, emerging from the tutelage of her grandmother and passing through the stage of doubt before she finally attains to the state of happiness. Veronica's progress, however, unlike that of so many of her predecessors in the *Bildungsroman*, is primarily of a spiritual nature, and its various stages are not marked by any involvements in exciting adventures.

When the novel opens Veronica is sixteen years old. Approaching maturity, she is beginning to become aware of disquieting discontent as she realizes that her life lacks an ethical center, lacks meaning. This highly susceptible and impressionable girl is open to many and varying influences from her immediate circle of relatives and friends. Her grandmother, with whom she lives, embodies a spirit of serene paganism, her aunt Edelgart is very strongly attracted by the Catholic faith, but has not that faculty of readiness to surrender the ego which a final commitment to Catholicism would demand and Enzio, the nearest to her in age, is a professed agnostic. These three very different personalities play important roles in Veronica's spiritual Odyssey, and her character and personality develop as she, in turn, becomes involved in the world of each of them.

The first steps in Veronica's progress are made under the tutelage of her grandmother against a background of the ruins and monuments of ancient Roman civilization. To the grandmother Rome represents the apogee of human achievement, the perennial symbol of the greatness and beauty which man can achieve by his own efforts. This is the concept of the city which she endeavors to impart to her young protégé and, for a time at least, it seems that she has been successful. Veronica appears to accept without question the pagan philosophy of her grandmother:

Casting aside the restricted limitations of my own unimportant ego. . . I, in those early years, made this immense city a part of myself, allowing my whole individuality to be submerged in it. My whole being became absorbed in its greatness and my personality expanded by contact with the plenitude of its glories and heroic figures.[2]

The period of Veronica's unquestioning acceptance of her grandmother's philosophy is of relatively short duration and terminates with the arrival of Enzio in the household.

The grandmother had taught Veronica to see Rome as the central point of the humanist world, but the young German, Enzio, very much a child of his age, approaches the city with vastly different expectations and demands. To him Rome is chiefly important as a visible symbol of the life processes of growth and decay, and he can muster little sympathy for what he regards as the old-world approach of the grandmother. Veronica's period of doubt begins when she becomes involved in the tension created by being confronted with these conflicting views of Rome, which represent two diametrically opposed concepts of human life and endeavor. During the course of the visit to the Forum Enzio's influence on Veronica begins to predominate over that of the grandmother. The noble columns, which the grandmother had represented as "marvellous intimations of an imperturbably serene majesty"[3] lose all their magic for Veronica when she re-visits them with Enzio. As he points out that these proud but impotent ruins have in reality no message for modern man, Veronica finds her loyalty to her grandmother's views weakening and an attraction for Enzio's forcefully-expressed ideas taking shape in her mind.

The culmination of Enzio's domination over Veronica's mind is marked by their visit to the moonlit Colosseum. In Enzio's company on this occasion Veronica sees the massive

ruins through his eyes as the epitome of his view of the whole
city, as the visible and abiding testimony of the bestial nature
of man, of his barbarity and inhumanity. The impression of
the Apollonian calm of the grandmother's Rome has now
been superseded by an uneasy awareness of the surging
Dionysian elements of Enzio's city. Veronica at this stage
feels herself to be "completely overshadowed by the dark
fluttering pinions of his spirit."[4] Yet the culminating point
of unity between Enzio and Veronica simultaneously marks
the point of divergence of their respective paths, and both
seek to come to terms with their experience in a characteristic manner. Enzio seeks release through the medium of art,
through his poetry; Veronica turns to a different level of
experience and seeks satisfaction in an entity outside her
own ego. Neither the Rome of the grandmother, the home
of classical art, the giver of form and beauty to temporal
phenomena, nor the Rome of Enzio, the city teeming with
life and redolent of decay, has fully satisfied Veronica. She
feels obscurely that a vital aspect of the city has somehow
eluded both her mentors, that her passage through their respective worlds has in effect been an "alienation of my own
personality."[5] Determined to discover for herself that elu-
sive aspect which she feels has somehow escaped both her
grandmother and Enzio, Veronica sets out alone to discover
yet another facet of the city, and so eventually finds herself
on the path to the Eternal City, the heart of Christendom.

The third and final stage in Veronica's progress may be
taken as beginning on her way home from the Colosseum.
Her path leads her past St. Peter's, and as the shadow of the
great dome encompasses her, Veronica suddenly has the sensation "as if I had traversed the whole universe and had now
arrived at its innermost heart."[6] She does not, however, as
yet rationalize this feeling, or even fully understand its implications, and has many obstacles to surmount before she

8

ultimately finds spiritual serenity. The decisive turning point in Veronica's life is marked by the Tenebrae service which she attends in St. Peter's in the company of her grandmother and Enzio. This represents her first encounter with the Passion Week liturgy of the Catholic Church, and the upheaval it induces in her soul is a portent of her subsequent conversion. Le Fort highlights the last transmutation in Veronica's spiritual progress by suggesting a parallel between the progressive darkening of the church during the service by the gradual extinguishing of all the lights, followed by their sudden restoration at the close, and Veronica's passage through the 'dark night of the soul' to the blinding clarity of faith. This moment of vision marks her attainment of that goal toward which she retrospectively sees her whole life to have been directed, and the novel ends with her formal reception into the Church.

The Roman fountain of the title has been used by le Fort as a symbol for the fate of her heroine, and may be looked on as an externalization of Veronica's subconscious longing. Its upsurging waters symbolize her spiritual aspirations and its murmur is paralleled within her heart by an inner urge to continue the quest which eventually leads her to happiness in acceptance of the Faith.

The portrait of the grandmother is perhaps the outstanding feature of *The Roman Fountain*. Apart from the important role she plays in Veronica's formative years, the grandmother's function in the story is important in its own right. Indeed, as the narrative progresses, the older woman's personality tends to overshadow her whole entourage. Le Fort limits the description of the physical appearance of the grandmother to the minimum, yet a striking portrait of an individual emerges; tall, dignified, affable, interested in the beauty of the world about her, attracted by the intelligent, but incapable of suffering fools gladly, and intolerant of mediocrity in all forms. Sentimentality, too, is anathema to her disciplined mind.

On the very first page we are told that the grandmother "used to assert with regard to herself that she was a pagan."[7] This introduction gives the keynote to her character and her approach to life. As the philosophic basis of her life the grandmother has accepted Descartes' *cogito, ergo sum*, and her trust and confidence in man as a self-sufficient and autonomous being is absolute. She lives her own life in complete accordance with her basic principles, in a context devoid of any transcendental connections or aspirations. Thus, even though she respects and honors the beliefs of others, she cannot herself admit the validity of any creed or code which would shift the axis of human life away from man and give the government of his life and destiny into the hands of some unknown and outside force. Within her self-imposed limitations the grandmother has attained a very high degree of that "serene greatness" which Winckelmann found reflected in ancient classical art.

In Rome the grandmother sees the incorporation of the noblest achievements of the human mind and heart. Its classical ruins represent for her an abiding testimony of man's potentialities and achievement, and she sees the city as "the marvellous symbol of earth's perennial greatness, the quintessence of humanity, which possesses the faculty of ennobling the individual."[8] In this city baseness has no place, and the atmosphere emanating from it ennobles and uplifts. Her mind feels a strong kinship with this treasure house of the past. She feels that here she has found her spiritual home, and, although a German by birth, has decided to spend her life in Rome: "Rome," she says, "is the natural habitat of form, and everything capable of being moulded into form assumes here the quality of immortality."[9]

It is possible that le Fort has imparted to the grandmother

many of the emotions which she herself experienced when in Rome, but her primary purpose in the portrayal of this character is to indicate the inadequacy of a purely humanist approach to life. The outward serenity and self-sufficiency of the old lady are accordingly shown to conceal a certain inability, or rather a refusal, to face the more disquieting facets of life in the city of her adoption. She habitually avoids the streets behind the Capitol, redolent of decay, which do not harmonize with her concept of the city as "the impregnable citadel of the centuries,"[10] and it is this facility to disregard what does not fit into her pre-conceived pattern that is in Enzio's mind when he perceptively remarks that the "grandmother underestimates the influence of Rome."[11] Similarly she refuses to take cognizance of any facts which would tend to refute her belief in the progressive advancement of the human race toward perfection, for in her eyes world history "appeared as an awe-inspiring triumphal progress of human greatness and immortality."[12]

The developing minds and characters of the two young people she loves, however, force the grandmother gradually to face those facts which, consciously or unconsciously, she had hitherto striven to ignore. The first undermining of her armor of imperturbability stems from Enzio. To this young man the grandmother has transferred some measure of the affection which she had once felt for his father, and has come to regard him with an almost maternal love. For some time she has been aware that he has been moving out of her intellectual orbit, and that certain aspects of Roman life which she refuses to contemplate seem actually to attract him. Enzio's eyes are fascinated not by the formal beauty of the great city, but by the chaotic forces which lie concealed and dormant behind the disciplined façade of its classical monuments. At first the grandmother optimistically forces herself to believe that this preoccupation of Enzio's is but a passing phase and that "her Rome would gradually become his and thus bring clarity to his mind."[13] This hope proves vain and actually blinds her to the fact that Enzio, as a representative of the modern post-Nietzschean generation, must necessarily react to Rome in a manner quite different from hers. When finally, Enzio comes to reveal his personal views in his poetry, it becomes apparent to her that he has in fact totally rejected the Rome to which she had so lovingly introduced him, and that such a rejection is tantamount to a complete repudiation of her whole philosophy of life. Her disappointment and grief are in proportion to the regard in which she has held him.

The grandmother characteristically conceals her feelings, but a second revelation, wounding her pride and self-esteem, is destined to sap still further her self-confidence. As a younger woman she had felt a great attraction for a married man, whose intellect matched her own and who had reciprocated her affection. Realizing that their relationship would wreck his marriage, she had decided that a great act of self-sacrifice and renunciation was the only procedure worthy of her, and all her life has rather prided herself on the nobility of her behavior in this crisis. Soon after her belated recognition of the true nature of Enzio's Roman experience, the interview with Enzio's mother, Frau Wolke, widow of the man who had inspired her affection, takes place. In the course of a violent altercation, Frau Wolke's smouldering resentment finds outlet at last in a series of vituperations which represent the grandmother's role in the earlier episodes from another angle. Frau Wolke's angry accusations force the grandmother to reassess her part in that far-distant episode, and she finds that she has long cherished the illusion of having been magnanimous and noble, whereas, viewed from the angle of the offended wife, her behavior was ignoble and despicable. The old lady's equilibrium is badly shaken as she must now see her whole subsequent life mirrored in another's hatred: "It was as if she had directed into her innermost heart a revealing flame which seared like red-hot iron a hidden area, to the existence of which, with all her nobility and her pride, she had never adverted, and the contemplation of it now in her old age made her shudder."[14] In this highly charged scene between the grandmother and Frau Wolke—a scene of great dramatic intensity—the very foundations on which her whole life had been built are undermined, and it is borne home to her that "even the noblest human being is blinded by self-interest."[15]

The last stage in the process of the grandmother's disillusionment is reached with Veronica's announcement of her intention to embrace the Catholic faith. This third blow is the most bitter of all as Veronica had always been "the one individual to whom she had always confided her deepest and noblest ideas, who, she believed, would always guard and keep within her heart everything pertaining to her own life which she considered worth perpetuating."[16] She views Veronica's intention to become a Catholic as the equivalent of a total rejection of the noble pagan ideals with which she had endeavored to imbue her, and her grandchild's defection—it amounts to such—as tantamount to her own complete failure to transmit to the next generation the values and ideals she cherished.

Instead of giving a lengthy description of the grandmother's chagrin and disappointment, le Fort uses a more subtle method. She represents the old lady, bravely concealing the shock to her pride and self-esteem, as setting out with Veronica on a series of last pilgrimages to her favorite shrines. But the old magic has vanished. The contemplation of the beauties of a dead age can now bring no serenity to the pilgrim's troubled soul; rather do they stir up a further undercurrent of disquiet. Their very aloofness and calm serve to stress their remoteness from the present, and reluctantly the grandmother must concede that "they are mere visitants to an age with which they no longer have anything inherently in common."[17] During these last days Veronica feels that her grandmother "was seeking something which she did not find,"[18] and that as they walked through the city they "were in Rome but not of it."[19]

The grandmother's life ends on a note of pathos. As her physical strength diminishes, she seeks in vain consolation from her earlier philosophy. Yet in spite of her spiritual desolation she utters no complaints, nor does she seek human sympathy. Her proud spirit upholds her to the end. She dies in a characteristically stoic manner, seated upright in her chair within sight of the Pantheon, epitome of all that she revered in Rome: "My grandmother died as proud and noble heroic figures die. She confronted death with dignity. She watched the relentless approach of this figure with the dark inscrutable eyes. With veiled head she accepted his presence, full of reverence, in complete silence, solitary and alone."[20] This stoic acceptance of death is not the consummation of a noble life, but rather the termination of a tenacious struggle against unequal odds. During her lifetime the grandmother had been able to present to the world a countenance reflecting serenity and peace of spirit, but on the dead face could be seen clearly etched the emotions of disappointment and sorrow she had so carefully struggled to conceal during her last days.

Whereas the grandmother is a timeless figure whose outlook is not conditioned by the age in which she lives, Enzio is essentially a modern character, an heir to the ideological world of Nietzsche and Kafka, one of the generation which has as yet found no substitute for the God it has rejected. The spirit of doubt and restlessness which characterizes this age is reflected in him and determines his view of life in all its manifestations. He approaches Rome from an angle very different from that of the grandmother and projects onto the city his own sense of restless dissatisfaction. As he has no positive ideological convictions, his world has no ethical center. When he looks at the Roman ruins, the grave of centuries, he feels an awareness of "concentrated darkness, a brooding silence exuding from below, horror, hidden forces, emanations, the restless swaying motion of amorphous masses."[21] This awareness of latent evil forces is not counterbalanced by the aspect of those ruins testifying to the glories of the past, and when he contemplates the chilly immutable grandeur of the Colosseum he is aware above all else of the impotence of the individual. These ruins gradually become equated in his mind with Rome itself and with the immutable laws of nature, and as he gazes in awe at them, he exclaims: "How awful is the face of Rome, for this is what it is. . . the Law and stone, stone and the Law, exactly like the world."[22] Their chilly silence disquiets him, imparting to him a feeling of utter desolation, and provoking in his mind doubts and questions about man's position in the scheme of things: "How desolate is man in the universe. This feeling of utter abandonment is strange, whence does it come?"[23]

To these questions his philosophy of life presents no satisfactory answer. The primeval, elemental forces of life, "this sublime and terrible thing, which gives being to all things and re-absorbs them,"[24] are continually uppermost in Enzio's consciousness, and he will admit of no transcendental connections they might conceivably have. This preoccupation with and awareness of the latent forces of corruption at the heart of things explain to a certain extent the peculiar fascination for Enzio of those aspects of Rome so distasteful to the grandmother. The dark streets behind the Pantheon and the fetid night air, redolent of the decay of centuries and the odor of chaos, obsess him as forcible reminders of the surging forces of life. Even the noble columns of the Forum, which to the grandmother are tangible expressions of grace and majesty, of human dignity, are to Enzio symbols of the eruptive forces which lie dormant beneath a serene exterior: "Even in the perfect form I am aware of what is behind and below, the horror of the deep and the giddiness of the heights, the constant rise and fall."[25]

In a manner characteristic of his generation Enzio turns from the realm of metaphysics and philosophy to the realm of art in his endeavors to come to terms with and give expression to his experience. His poetry, the chosen medium of his artistic consciousness, is consequently not an externalization of an inner peace and harmony, but rather an affirmation of "the ultimate unreality of all things,"[26] of the Rome that he has assimilated as a symbol of the "ghostly nature of all existence."[27] His poetry has a catalytic function insofar as it helps to crystallize his experience in artistic terms, yet it cannot offer him a solution to his personal problems, and as a man his personal stature fails to keep pace with his development as a poet. Enzio's problem is in effect one that is very much in the artistic consciousness of our times, one that figures prominently in the work of such writers as Thomas Mann and Franz Kafka: it is the dual problem of the dichotomy between the artist and the man, and of the integration of the artist in society. In the case of Enzio this dichotomy is increased by virtue of his own awareness of it and his inability to evolve a solution: "It is most difficult of all for the artist to achieve spiritual liberation, or even to become a full personality, because he constantly finds in his art a spurious liberation and an illusion of reality."[28] Enzio's major fear is that his poetry will become a substitute for life, that he will ultimately cease to be vibrantly alive and will become the prey and victim of his own imaginative powers: "The poet's life is an untrammelled existence, but frequently it is not the life that he as a man would like to lead."[29] *The Roman Fountain* depicts Enzio with the dichotomy between his life and his art as yet unresolved: qualities seen here in embryo are further developed in the sequel, *The Wreath of Angels,* in which Enzio again plays a leading role.

The city of Rome does not merely supply the background of the story but, as we have seen, has been very skillfully integrated with the development of the characters. Rome exercises a formative influence on the lives of main protagonists, orienting or confirming the direction of their respective lives, so that one might almost speak of the city's playing a decisive role in the action. In effect it dominates the whole narrative. Multifarious aspects of the many-sided city have been vividly and graphically brought to life and the respective reactions of the main characters to its attractions provide an interesting illustration of the Thomistic axiom that everything enters the mind according to the mind of the receiver. Thus the grandmother, Enzio and Veronica are respectively attuned to perceive the classical grandeur of the monuments, the chaotic disorder of the ruins and the spiritual significance of the Eternal City, and their individual destinies have been fashioned by their spiritual and intellectual affinity with the varying aspects of this city of their adoption.

By contrast with the main characters the three minor characters do not really come to life, and in the ultimate analysis they are introduced mainly to elaborate le Fort's ideas. Of the three, Veronica's Aunt Edelgart is the most important, and le Fort devotes an undue proportion of the story to her and to her problems. Edelgart is a neurotic, unbalanced character who continually hankers after spiritual security. Although she intellectually assents to the beliefs of Catholicism, some strange inhibition prevents her from following the logical course open to her. In le Fort's view, Edelgart's inability to surrender the ego to a Superior Being is the besetting sin of the present age. Edelgart is an unattractive figure, but she gives expression to some of le Fort's views on certain aspects of religion and its role in man's life—in particular on the efficacy of prayer and the theme of responsibility on a spiritual level—and, although she remains unconvincing as a personality, on these grounds her role is not without importance.

To Jeanette, Veronica's former governess who has stayed on in the household, is assigned the role of a confidante for the views and beliefs of main characters. She, the only member of the household to admit of and subscribe to a supernatural reality, embodies the virtues of the true Christian. Her whole life is an expression of the principle on which her life is based, *adoro, ergo sum,* and her simplicity and unquestioning faith stand in marked contrast to the intellectual preoccupations and worries of the other characters.

The third minor character, Enzio's mother, known as Frau Wolke, is but lightly sketched. For Frau Wolke, who seems in almost every respect to be the antithesis of her gifted son, Rome holds neither an intellectual nor a spiritual attraction. She, in marked contrast to all the others, feels ill at ease with what she terms this "tête-à-tête with world history and with matters pertaining to eternity."[30] Material well being is the only standard that has any meaning to her and she is the epitome of that "respectable middle class" (solide Bürgertum) so despised by her artistic son. Frau Wolke, however, is not introduced as a mere foil for the other characters, but contributes in no small measure to the undermining of the grandmother's equanimity and the ultimate pathetic collapse of her world. The name by which she is introduced is not without significance. Like a dark cloud (Wolke) she casts a shadow over the sunny philosophy of the grandmother, and the echo of her accusations intensifies the gloom of the latter's last days on earth.

The title under which *The Roman Fountain* was originally published, *The Veil of Veronica*, would seem to indicate that the main interest of the novel was intended to be the development of the character and the unfolding of the fate of the heroine under the influence of her grandmother, Enzio and her aunt. In the course of the narrative, however, the grandmother and Enzio evolve into such forceful personalities that they tend to overshadow and eclipse the somewhat insubstantial heroine, with the result that they become rival claimants for the reader's attention and interest. This results in one of the main technical weaknesses of the novel, namely, the swift transitions from the problems of one of the main characters to those of the others. These transitions tend to disrupt the flow of the narrative and to sidetrack the reader's attention. There is, of course, another very important factor to be taken into account when assessing this novel, namely, the fact that in 1928 le Fort was as yet without experience in the art of novel writing. As she later gained greater experience she overcame many of the difficulties which confronted her in her first novel. A brief outline of some of these difficulties will serve to indicate the source of its main weaknesses.

By choosing to narrate the story in the autobiographical form le Fort was faced with the first major difficulty, that of presenting a serious theme through the medium of an immature adolescent who is directly involved in the events she narrates. Her efforts to make Veronica's deductions and comments more credible have not been wholly successful and such devices as the heroine reporting conversations which she has overheard unseen and her ability to divine the thought processes of other characters strike the reader as being somewhat contrived. In *The Roman Fountain* le Fort has not completely mastered the difficulties presented by her chosen form; in its sequel, *The Wreath of Angels*, we shall see how her technical skill has increased in this respect.

Le Fort's aims and intentions in writing *The Roman Fountain* presented a second major difficulty: they also proved
prejudicial to a well-knit structure. At no stage was she concerned to write a novel of action, whose focus would be on
external events or on the human repercussions of such events,
but from the outset she concentrated on the gradual unfolding and development of the minds and personalities of the
main characters. There is, accordingly, much emphasis on
thought processes and ideas, and the resultant long passages
of psychical analysis and reflection, fundamental though
these are to the development of the theme, tend to slow up
the action. The lack of a division into chapters has also con-
tributed to the tendency to diffuseness.

When discussing the stylistic weaknesses of *The Roman
Fountain* it is relevant to recall the date of its publication.
In 1928, when it appeared, a psychological novel which at-
tempted to portray an interior spiritual progress was a relatively new departure in Germany. It demanded a new approach to storytelling—or at least a modification of established techniques—and faced le Fort with the difficult task
of breaking new literary ground or of adapting an outworn
technique to a new type of subject matter. Since she was then
at the very beginning of her career as a novelist and had
neither the ability nor the stature of such writers as James
Joyce and Virginia Woolf, who so brilliantly pioneered the
"stream of consciousness" technique in the English-speaking
world, le Fort was not wholly successful in mastering the
difficulties with which she was presented. In *The Roman
Fountain*, she arrived at what is in effect an uneasy compromise between form and content.

On the positive side, this novel is characterized by a direct,
evocative and uncomplicated use of language, and le Fort's
descriptive gifts, together with her facility in suggesting atmosphere, are seen here to good effect. The graphic evoca-

tion of many aspects of the Roman scene bear witness to this aspect of her talent: the visit of Enzio and Veronica to the moonlit Colosseum, the description of the Tenebrae service at St. Peter's, and the account of final days and death of the grandmother, passages all very different in character, give a measure of her versatility and ability to convey atmosphere.

On balance *The Roman Fountain* is an uneven work. Lengthy explanations of spiritual and psychological problems of limited appeal stand side by side with exciting and effective descriptive passages; the treatment of the theme is original, yet le Fort's concern for lucidity often results in a loss in subtlety. This work is interesting as a record of an early phase in le Fort's development as a novelist and of her treatment of religious and spiritual problems, but it was destined to be surpassed in literary merit by much of her subsequent work, where her enthusiastic commitment is more happily reconciled with the demands of good fiction.

CHAPTER I

1. English translation, *The Veil of Veronica* (London, 1932).
2. Losgelöst von den allzu engen Schranken meines kleinen Ich...
   fing mein junges Leben diese unermessliche Stadt auf, indem es
   selbst von ihr aufgefangen wurde: eingetaucht in ihre Grösse,
   ausgeweitet in die Fülle ihrer Gestalten und Herrlichkeiten.
   Schriften I, p. 27.
3. Wundervolle Andeutungen einer unerschütterlichen Majestät.
   Schriften I, p. 70.
4. Erfasst von den dunklen gebrochenen Flügeln seines Geistes.
   Schriften I, p. 149.
5. Eine Entfremdung meiner selbst. *Ibid.*, p. 149.
6. Als wäre ich durch die ganze Welt gegangen und stünde nun
   vor ihrem innersten Herzen. *Schriften I*, p. 152.
7. Meine Grossmutter behauptete von sich selbst, dass sie eine
   Heidin sei. *Schriften I*, p. 7.
8. Das wundervolle Symbol irdischer Grösse und Ewigkeit, die
   Zusammenfassung der Menschheit und die Erhöherin der eigenen Person. *Schriften I*, p. 213.

9. Rom sei eine grosse Heimat der Form, und alles, was überhaupt die Fähigkeit habe, gestaltet zu werden, das werde hier auch zur unverlierbaren Gestalt. *Ibid.*, p. 265.

10. Die unbezwingbare Hochburg der Jahrtausende. *Schriften* I, p. 61.

11. Dass meine Grossmutter Rom zu harmlos nehme. *Ibid.*, p. 64.

12. Erschien (ihr) wie ein erhabener Triumphzug menschlicher, Grösse und Unsterblichkeit. *Ibid.*, p. 23.

13. Ihr Rom werde allmählich das seine und damit ihn selbst klären. *Schriften* I, p. 171.

14. Es war, als senke sie eine schmerzlich helle Flamme tief in ihr Inneres hinab und brenne wie mit glühendem Eisen eine verborgene Stelle darinnen auf, zu der sie mit all ihrem Edelmut, mit all ihrer Grösse und Gerechtigkeit, ja selbst mit all ihrem Stolz noch niemals hingeblickt hatte, und vor der sie nun als alte Frau noch erbebte. *Schriften* I, p. 251.

15. Auch der edelste Mensch in Schuld verstrickt ist. *Ibid.*, p. 266.

16. Der Mensch, dem sie ihr Tiefstes und Bestes vertraut hatte, in dessen Seele sie alles niedergelegt und treu bewahrt glaubte, was ihr aus dem eigenen Sein würdig erschienen, dass es weitergetragen werde. *Ibid.*, p. 280.

17. Gäste einer Zeit, mit der sie im Innersten nichts mehr gemein hatten. *Schriften* I, p. 269, 270.

18. Dass sie im Grunde etwas suchte, was sie nicht fand. *Ibid.*, p. 266.

19. Als gingen wir mitten in Rom immerfort an Rom vorüber. *Ibid.*, p. 268.

20. Meine Grossmutter starb, wie stolze und edle Helden sterben. Ihr Tod war antlitzhaft und erhaben. Sie sah ihn bewusst auf sich zuschreiten als eine schwermütige Gestalt mit dunklem, unergründlichem Blick. Sie empfing ihn verhüllten Hauptes, ehrfürchtig und vollkommen schweigend, ganz einsam. *Schriften* I, p. 282.

21. Zusammenballungen, dunkel Emporschweigendes, Schauer, Gewalten, Ergossenheiten, das ruhelose Schweben dessen, was nicht mehr Gestalt ist. *Schriften* I, p. 62.

22. Wie schauerlich ist das Antlitz Roms, denn dieses ist es. . . Gesetz und Stein, Stein und Gesetz, geradeso ist diese Welt. *Ibid.*, p. 146.

23. Wie verlassen ist der Mensch im Universum. . . Dieses Verlassenheitsgefühl ist so merkwürdig-woher haben wir es nur? *Ibid.*, pp. 146, 147.

24. Dieses prachtvolle und schaurige Ding, welches alles aus sich emportreibt und alles in sich zurückschlingt. *Schriften* I, p. 72.

Gertrud von le Fort

25. Ich fühle auch im Vollendeten noch das Dahinter und Darunter, das Grausen der Tiefe und den Schwindel der Höhe, das Immer-wieder-Hinauf-und-Hinab! *Ibid.*, p. 72.
26. Jener letzten Unwirklichkeit aller Dinge. *Schriften*, I, p. 203.
27. Der Spukhaftigkeit des gesamten Seins. *Ibid.*, p. 205.
28. Der Künstler (kann) am schwersten erlöst werden oder auch nur Persönlichkeit sein, weil er immerfort die Scheinerlösung und die Scheingestalt in seiner Kunst hat. *Ibid.*, p. 254.
29. Dichten ist. . . ein ganz starkes, wildes Leben. . . Aber manchmal ist es gar nicht das Leben, das man gerade als Mensch leben möchte. *Schriften* I, p. 97.
30. Diese tete-à-tete mit der Weltgeschichte und den ewigen Dingen. *Schriften* I, p. 59.

CHAPTER II

The Wreath of Angels

An interval of almost twenty years separates the publication of *The Roman Fountain* from that of its sequel, *The Wreath of Angels*. However, as the two novels deal with the same characters and have since been published together under the title *The Veil of Veronica* (1956), it is more convenient to consider the later novel here than to let the sequence be determined by publication dates alone.

The Wreath of Angels takes as its main theme what Goethe once described as the most profound theme of world history, namely, the conflict between the forces of good and evil, between belief and disbelief. Le Fort sets this perennial struggle in a modern context and the action of the novel, which revolves around the encounter between the Christian Veronica and the pagan Enzio, takes place in Germany in the early 1920's. In the pages of this novel le Fort broaches questions of a fundamental nature to anyone concerned with such problems as that of the relationship between the Christian and the non-Christian in the modern world. Does the believer share a responsibility for the fate of the unbeliever and, if so, has he a duty to take steps to impart to others his own convictions about ultimate values? What should be the

attitude of the Christian in face of active and violent oppo-
sition to his faith and how, can he best maintain his position
in such a situation?

Le Fort approaches these various problems as a convert to
Catholicism who feels deeply that in the modern tendency
to divorce life from its divine origins lies the root of many
of the ills with which the world has been visited in recent
times. She develops these views here in the specific context
of a Germany where Nazism was beginning to take hold,
and links the disregard for individual liberty evinced under
the Nazi regime with man's endeavor to cut God out of his
life and demonstrate his complete autonomy. In such a situation she believes the only effective action on the part of
the believing Christian to lie in a readiness to make sacrifices in order that unbelievers may be saved.

In *The Wreath of Angels* these questions of the Christian's
responsibility in present-day society are very closely linked
with the problem of evil. Here the emergence of the forces
of evil is depicted in a period when Germany was still smart-
ing under defeat and the Treaty of Versailles; it is seen under the guise of an emergent new nationalism—Nazism. In
contrast to *The Roman Fountain*, where the themes were
developed in a context unrelated to social or political conditions, *The Wreath of Angels* links its main themes intimately with the specific period in which the story is set.

The narrator-heroine of *The Wreath of Angels* is again
Veronica, and the novel begins with her arrival at Heidelberg
to pursue her studies at the university. The connection with
The Roman Fountain is established at the outset and the reader unfamiliar with the earlier work is quickly made acquaint-
ed with what is relevant to an understanding of the characters and events. The action of the novel is engaged when
Veronica meets in Heidelberg Enzio, who had been her girl-
hood friend in Rome, and the professor, who was appointed

her guardian after the deaths of her grandmother and aunt, in whose house she has now come to make her home.

The first part of the novel, dealing with the growing love between Veronica and Enzio, has many aspects of the conventional love story. The city of Heidelberg, home of the Romantics, provides a suitably idyllic background to the action, and the language, colored by the subjective emotions of the narrator, tends to be rather sentimental in character. As the story progresses, however, it becomes clear that this is not just another run-of-the-mill love story and that Veronica's love for Enzio has a quality and significance differentiating it from the usual emotional involvement. *The Roman Fountain* ended with Veronica's conversion to Catholicism, an event destined to have a decisive effect on her character and on the subsequent course of her life. She has now arrived in Heidelberg with a sense of mission and an awareness of being mystically united with her patron saint Veronica, and like her, she too is desirous of showing to the world the face of Christ. In this frame of mind she again encounters Enzio who, in the intervening years, has become a complete pagan. With her new-found sense of mission in life Veronica feels a responsibility for his spiritual destiny, and her love for him becomes mystical in nature: "I who love God am the object of Enzio's love, therefore he loves God through me,"[1] she reasons. In the bond of this love which unites her to Enzio Veronica sees his sole remaining link with his Creator; she is determined that this link must not be severed, whatever the cost.

In the course of the latter part of this novel the romantic elements give way to a decided emphasis on the religious-mystical aspects of the heroine's experience. The visit of Veronica and Enzio to Speyer marks the point where this change in emphasis begins to make itself felt. In its ancient, historic cathedral, where Enzio implicitly refuses to agree to a Christian marriage within the Church, the extreme polarity of their respective concepts of love becomes apparent to Veronica. This discovery is not, however, the prelude to the breaking-off of the engagement. Veronica sees in Enzio's complete estrangement from God and from the Church a compulsive reason for staying at his side. Her line of argument is that "the fact that he is estranged from God is the very reason that you cannot now abandon him, for God Himself does not abandon those souls which abjured Him, but rather does He pursue them and love them in Christ."[2] From this point onward Veronica's relationship with Enzio is essentially mystical rather than emotional, and the motivation for her action throughout the remainder of the novel assumes a religious rather than a psychological character.

Veronica's struggle against the powerful will of Enzio, who seeks to undermine her faith and to force her into a non-sacramental marriage with him, now becomes the focal point of interest. This struggle begins when Enzio's hatred of religion and of all pertaining to it begins to become vocal. His writings become openly anti-religious and, though he still loves her after his fashion, he makes no secret of his views to Veronica. Despite this, however, Veronica's determination to save his soul never wavers and she resolves never to forsake him, even though the execution of such a resolve might necessitate a marriage outside her Church.

In the long struggle to adhere to her resolution and to withstand the force of Enzio's strong will, Veronica finds herself completely isolated, the only character with any sympathy for her attitude being her former spiritual advisor, Father Angelo, who lives in Rome and communicates with her by letter. In his letters Fr. Angelo expresses in general terms his views on the alternative methods of dealing with antagonism to the Faith: "There is a natural and a supernatural approach to those who have become the enemies of

God. The former is to sever all connection with the sinner in order to safeguard one's own salvation, the supernatural way is to cleave to him."[3] Of these two possible courses, the second, being the one in harmony with Veronica's character, is the one which she adopts. She interprets Fr. Angelo's words as an 'absolute command' to keep her resolution even though her confessor, the deacon, counsels her to dissociate her life from that of Enzio. In her efforts to save Enzio's soul she ultimately foregoes even the spiritual consolation of the sacraments of the Church.[4] The intensity of her struggle against Enzio brings Veronica to the point of an almost complete physical collapse, but her efforts finally meet with at least a measure of success. As the book ends with her moral triumph over the power of evil represented by her adversary, the reader deduces that Enzio will henceforth respect, if not share, Veronica's beliefs.

The above outline of the relationship between Enzio and Veronica will have made it obvious that le Fort's main concern was not to describe the tortuous details of a romantic attachment but to trace the development of a spiritual relationship, and that she has used the heroine to stress the value of vicarious suffering and to emphasize the importance of *caritas* in human relationships. As a consequence of this eagerness to illustrate an idea, le Fort has not succeeded in making the character of her heroine wholly convincing, and as the action advances and the author becomes increasingly engrossed in the elucidation of her themes, the weaknesses in characterization increase. Reflections and discussions of matters of purely confessional interest assume undue prominence, and the reader feels that Veronica is becoming more and more divorced from reality. In *The Wreath of Angels*, as in *The Roman Fountain*, the portrait of the heroine is one of the least satisfying features of the novel.

Enzio—though he too is not without symbolic significance

as the symbol of the force against which Veronica struggles —strikes the reader as being far more true to life than the heroine. The Enzio of *The Roman Fountain* with his restless questing spirit now belongs to the past. His first words are indicative of the change that has taken place in him: "Rome is a thing of the past. Now comes Germany. . . Germany's fate has become indissolubly linked with mine."[5] In Rome he had felt the absence of a metaphysical center to his life, had experienced what he described as a "deep dread of spiritual abandonment."[6] Since those days, however, World War I has intervened and Enzio's speculative interest in metaphysics has been replaced by a new ideology. He has cast aside religion and everything pertaining to it with the assertion that "religion no longer plays a role in my life. As far as I am concerned it does not exist."[7] For those who cherish and preserve the religious and cultural heritage of the past he has only arrogant contempt, and he concentrates all his energies on the realization of his new ideal, the re-establishment of German might and power. He sees it "as the one great task confronting him, as his own particular mission in life, to abandon this fruitless obsession with the past and to set up a new, simple, practical, easily comprehensible truth to which one could adhere and according to whose tenets one could live."[8] Anything threatening to obstruct or hinder the realization of his ideal must, in Enzio's view, be immediately and ruthlessly crushed. He regards religion as possessing such a potential and therefore strives to exclude anything savoring of it from his relationship with Veronica. He maintains that "as long as man feels dependent on a higher power he does not stake his all, and complete and unreserved dedication is essential to my work. An unprecedented expansion in the might of our people must take place and I have no intention of tolerating any attempt to curb this development."[9]

Enzio is one of those "who have never come to terms with

the failure of the war. He would never intellectually accept its tragic end and still waged it in his mind."[10] Refusing to accept the reality of defeat, he concentrates all his energies on the building-up of a new future for his country and comes to see it as his personal mission "to free the people from this dreadful peace."[11]

He gives verbal expression to his aims in polemical essays, and hopes to propagate his ideas through the medium of his journalistic activity. Prose rather than poetry seems the more suitable medium for the expression of his views, and he considers the mellifluous verses which had intoxicated him in Rome to be now outmoded: the poet in him has given place to the forward-looking man of action.

The visit to Speyer, which marks Veronica's realization of the gulf which separates their two words, is of great importance for an understanding of Enzio's character. In its ancient cathedral, to Enzio "an expression of the majesty of the Reich,"[12] he first speaks explicitly to her about what he believes to be his personal mission and about the mighty power of the future, the new Reich. There he tells her that "he was not merely concerned with the emergence of our nation from its bitter plight; what he envisaged was the prescriptive right of our people, transcending time—the glory of the old empire."[13] The goal in Enzio's mind bears little relation to that of "the holy Roman empire of the German people"; his empire is to be set in an exclusively secular context, completely divorced from any of the spiritual associations to which the cathedral at Speyer is a monument:

> This kingdom is eternal. In my kingdom there will be no sacraments. . . There will only be victor and vanquished. There can never be any question of reconciliation between the nations. How could any nation concern itself with a God in whose sight all nations are brothers? In my kingdom there will be crowns of victory.[14]

To bring his concept to fulfillment Enzio relies on the strength of his will, which he regards as an autonomous absolute. He is convinced that "we are capable of doing anything we are determined to do and what we make up our minds to do lies within our physical capacity."[15] One of the most striking features of this portrait is the manner in which Enzio's will gradually assumes complete control over his personality until he ultimately arrives at a point where he can no longer control it. Features hitherto not manifest in his character begin to emerge, notably a complete ruthlessness and a total disregard for any persons or things which threaten to obstruct him in the pursuit of his aims.

At first glance the complete *volte face* may seem unconvincing, but the perceptive reader will realize that those characteristics which now distinguish Enzio had existed during his Roman sojourn, although they were then only in an embryonic or latent state and will recall that even there the young poet had emphasized that he considered art to be less important than living. It is not therefore really surprising that Enzio should now abandon the poet's vicarious form of life in favor of firsthand experience. When viewed in this light his final harsh treatment of Veronica and the professor is not the result of a sudden transformation in his character, but rather the culmination of a slow and gradual development.

This portrait of Enzio may help us to understand something of the mentality induced by Nazism. The individual caught in the soul-destroying system loses all power of volition, becoming a mere automaton blindly obeying an external force, incapable of shaking off the shackles of a monster he has helped to create.[16] A deeper significance may be seen in the portrait if it is regarded as an exposition of the consequences resulting from a willful severing of all connection with the supernatural and from an alliance with the forces of evil. Such an alliance, le Fort suggests, amounts to the possession of the individual by a positive force which takes control of his will and directs his action, and on a large scale it can lead to a dehumanization of a whole people and to a full-scale destruction of accepted norms of behavior and values.

While le Fort has portrayed in Enzio the Nazi mentality, in the professor and the minor characters she analyzes some aspects of the intellectual background of the period immediately preceding the emergence of Nazism. The professor stands as representative of the intelligentsia of that time, and through him le Fort gives us her interpretation of the failure of the intellectual leaders, who were among the few groups in a position to assess at the outset its destructive potential, and to effectively stem the course of Nazism. In the professor we have a highly effective character study combined with a perceptive analysis of the spiritual bankruptcy of the intelligentsia.

The professor—like the grandmother in *The Roman Fountain* he is given no proper name—incorporates the best features of the German man of letters, the 'academicus,' and his unassuming, yet compelling, personality reflects his powerful intellect. The professor is depicted as being much preoccupied with the idea of the interdependence of Christianity and Western civilization and culture.[17] Christianity, in his view, is the cornerstone of our civilization, "the creative principle of our culture, its source and promise of the future, its unity in diversity,"[18] and he is gravely disturbed by the disrespect and disregard for their traditional faith evinced by his students. He is convinced that the contemporary decline in faith must inevitably have a deleterious effect on the culture with which it is indissolubly linked: "the betrayal of religion will have as a necessary corollary the betrayal of culture. The span of life of our Western civilization will be determined by the duration of the life of Western religion.

It is not the former which upholds the latter, but the latter the former."[19] Acutely conscious that he is living through a crucial turning point in history, the professor takes a pessimistic view of its outcome. He sees his own age as the dim twilight marking the close of that bright splendor which characterized the age of European Christian civilization and believes that it is true that "one can live for a while in the glow of a great sunset, but only for a while. The setting of the sun is of its nature a transient phenomenon. When the evening sky glows, the sun has already set."[20] His premonition that the emergence of a new dawn will occur only "after a tragedy of unimaginable dimensions"[21] is destined to become a sad reality.

Convincing though the professor may sound in the lecture hall, his eloquence is not informed by firmly-held convictions and in effect he epitomizes the dilemma of the modern intellectual; he combines a profound respect for religion and its educative power with a basic philosophic uncertainty. He is without effective weapons to resist the onslaught of the destructive forces he sees advancing, and also without the power to convince his students of the importance of preserving their inheritance. They are quick to divine that no positive personal commitment lies behind his trenchant statements and are not convinced of the urgency of his message. They are attracted by the mystique of patriotism proclaimed with such fervor by Enzio, and ultimately spurn completely the cultural heritage which the professor tries to pass on to them. He is fated to see his cherished ideals rejected, to realize that Enzio, in whom he had seen his most gifted student "had only attended his lectures in order to acquire the weapons to overthrow him,"[22] and that the students, in whom he had placed his confidence as preservers of the values dear to him, are no more independent of thought than the masses "who are incapable of resistance and will succumb to Enzio's ideology like tools, incapable of thought in unscrupulous hands."[23] As he leaves the arena, an aging man, Nemesis overtakes him, and he sees himself fated to play the role of a helpless bystander and passively watch the rise of a force which, he suspects, will precipitate the spiritual and intellectual bankruptcy of his country. Although the portrait of the professor is drawn with sympathy, his values, like those of the grandmother in *The Roman Fountain*, are shown to be inadequate. The analogy between these two figures is in fact quite striking. Both appear in the role of Veronica's guardian; both endeavor to transmit to her their own philosophy of life, and though she respects them, Veronica ultimately follows only the path which her own conscience and sensibility indicate. The parallel may be further developed in their respective relations with Enzio. Both share an illusory hope that Enzio will be their spiritual and intellectual heir, and both live to see him develop along lines antithetical to all their ideals. Through the characters of Enzio and the professor the second theme of the novel has been developed from two perspectives, and le Fort has outlined the salient features of the Nazi mentality and pointed to one of the basic reasons for its rapid and successful rise to power.

In Enzio's friend Starossow le Fort aims at indicating the manner in which so many Germans became enmeshed in the toils of the Nazi machine. By their initial failure to assert their independence of thought they were gradually caught up and engulfed in a current so overwhelming in force that it deprived them of the ability to offer any effective resistance to it. Such is the fate of Starossow, a man of malleable and pliant character, who has been intellectually devoured by the strong-willed Enzio. Starossow has been conditioned by Enzio until he has become a mere reflex and echo of his masterful friend; he is no more than a puppet, whose strings the stronger personality may manipulate at will.

The professor's wife, known as Frau Seide, and Enzio's mother, Frau Wolke, epitomize the bourgeois[24] spirit and outlook. Both are complete materialists, uninterested in and incapable of seeing anything in a context other than that of their own lives. Of the two, Frau Seide is portrayed in greater detail and has the more important part to play. To Seide life is a continuous theatrical performance, in which she herself is the leading actress. She reduces everything and everybody to the dimensions of theatrical props, whose value is judged by one criterion only, their potential usefulness as a foil to her own performance. Viewing all things and people in relation only to herself, Seide has no interest in people as individuals, and accordingly there is not and cannot be any real communication between her and those with whom she lives. She is totally lacking in that generosity of spirit which makes genuine friendship possible. The perfection of the façade presented by Seide serves to conceal a complete lack of depth and a dissembling and unreliable nature, and her character is aptly summed up in Enzio's remark: "everything pertaining to her is merely a beautiful camouflage."[25]

In Frauen Seide and Wolke le Fort portrays the mentality of a large section of the community whose empty and meaningless lives are completely devoid of any spiritual aspirations or connections. They are incapable of any profundity of thought, unconcerned with any wider interests, incapable of "seeing life steadily and seeing it whole." Unaware of the dangers which may be looming ahead, they play out their shallow existence on life's stage and are easy victims of those avid of power who exploit them for their own ends.

In any work with a claim to literary merit a high degree of intimacy will exist between the theme and the form in which it finds its expression: the form will not be superimposed from without, but will spring naturally from the subject matter. Despite its weaknesses, such an intimacy exists in *The Wreath of Angels* and will be apparent from a consideration of the symbolism employed. Le Fort, concerned primarily with psychological and spiritual matters, is confronted with the problem of how best to give these expression. She has developed and expanded her themes with the aid of symbolism and, while it may be argued that this novel can be validly interpreted as a simple story of human relationships, it takes on a new dimension if we view the characters and events in a symbolic context.

The characters of *The Wreath of Angels* may be regarded as symbols in the wider connotation of the word. As indicated above, the heroine and hero symbolize the forces of good and evil respectively; the professor, Seide and Wolke symbolize various levels of the bourgeois mind, and in the two minor figures of Fr. Angelo and the deacon, two aspects of the Church, the mystical and the practical, are represented. Similarly, the relationship between the characters has a symbolic function, and the struggle between Veronica and Enzio is symbolic of that between good and evil, and, more particularly, of the relationship between the believer and the unbeliever.

The formal connection between *The Wreath of Angels* and *The Roman Fountain* will be immediately apparent. Both are written in the autobiographical form and have a common narrator-heroine, and both feature the activities of the same characters. The manner in which the themes are presented is likewise common to the two novels as is the lack of a structural division into chapters. Apart from these immediately apparent similarities, an intimate stylistic relationship exists between the two works: we shall briefly examine this relationship in respect to the use of imagery.

The images used in both novels fit into a discernible pattern. They are limited in number and tend to recur frequently. These images may be conveniently divided into four groups: i) images of a *nautical* nature; ii) images relating to *light;* iii) images pertaining to a *bird* in flight; iv) images which are linked by a *unity of purpose* rather than by a verbal connection. The image of a ship is used in both novels in a descriptive capacity. Rome is described as "a large grey ship, anchored peacefully in the noonday,"[26] and, in *The Wreath of Angels*, Heidelberg is described in similar terms: "like a highly-colored, high-masted ship lying at anchor with its silver keel touching the sea below."[27]

The light image, used extensively at the beginning of *The Wreath of Angels*, has been directly taken up from the pages of *The Roman Fountain* and takes on added significance as a leitmotif. In *The Roman Fountain*, Veronica expressed her wish to save Enzio from the depressing consequences of his gloomy thoughts in the words: "I had the feeling that I had to hold my soul in my hand as if it were a little candle so that he could be brought to a belief in the existence of his own soul."[28] In *The Wreath of Angels*, this phrase is repeated by her in a similar context: "I had the illusion of holding my soul in my hand like a little candle, for his face lit up as if illumined by its rays."[29] The thread of this image is immediately followed up in Enzio's response: "so you have come here to bring light to me?"[30]

The relevance of this much-repeated image of light to one of the main themes of the novel, Veronica's view of her relationship with Enzio as a personal mission for the salvation of his soul, is made clear for the reader through a remark of Enzio's: "You stand up there like a candle in your white dress, while all about me there is darkness. Will you not come down and bring me light?"[31] By this remark he unwittingly adverts to what Veronica feels to be her particular role in life—to illuminate by the light of her own faith the darkness of Enzio's sceptical mind. An extension of this image is used with reference to Enzio, but in this latter context it has undergone a significant change. The power of his will is likened to a "magnetic current."[32] This current is in essence quite different from the soft beam of a candle: its harsh effulgence, coupled with its strong magnetic power, can overpower and subjugate the beholder.

The image of the bird, less striking than the image of light, has also been directly taken up from *The Roman Fountain*. It occurs in both novels, mainly with reference to Veronica's facility in detaching herself from her immediate surroundings and in becoming totally absorbed in a world of ideas. In the Colosseum Enzio likened Veronica to a bird poised for flight; after the professor's lecture she seems to him to be similarly ready to take flight into the ideological world of another, and here he explicitly refers to the earlier occasion: "we used to say that you were like a bird. . . Are you still poised for flight as you were in those days?"[33] Later in *The Wreath of Angels* this image is used without reference to the earlier context and Veronica's recovery from her illness and her return to a more balanced outlook on life are represented in a similar manner: "I recovered gradually. . . as if my spirit were returning from an immeasurable distance, but with broken wings."[34]

The images of the fourth group are not centered around any one specific object: they may be treated as a group by virtue of their common function, which is to indicate the gradual undermining of Veronica's personality in the clash with Enzio. These images, often suggestive of the weird and uncanny, show a striking connection with those used to describe the breakdown of Edelgart in *The Roman Fountain*. When Veronica comes under the domination of the demonic power represented in Enzio's will she is described as moving "like a ghost around an empty house,"[35] which is an exact repetition of the image used to describe Edelgart. The use of this imagery culminates in the description of Veronica's nightmares, "these eerie moonlit illuminations of a strange world,"[36] and these too are reminiscent of the images used to depict Edelgart's experiences.

The close and subtly developed unity between *The Roman Fountain* and *The Wreath of Angels,* to which we have pointed, leads the critic to surmise that the eighteen-year gap between their respective dates of publication does not apply to their dates of composition. This supposition seems all the more likely to be correct if we bear in mind that it would scarcely have been prudent—if indeed possible—to publish between 1933 and 1945 a novel like *The Wreath of Angels,* which conceals under a very thin disguise an indictment of the intellectual background of the Nazi ideology. It is possible that *The Wreath of Angels* was conceived, and perhaps partially drafted, very soon after *The Roman Fountain* and that many aspects of the plot—in particular the depiction of Enzio's fanaticism—were filled in in greater detail during the period when the threat of Nazi supremacy had become a bitter reality in Germany. Its publication in 1946 immediately after the collapse of the Nazi regime would seem to further substantiate our supposition.

On the final analysis *The Wreath of Angels,* like *The Roman Fountain,* must be adjudged to be a work in which le Fort has permitted her eagerness to propound her themes to take precedence over the demands of the novel as an art form. The heroine's preoccupation with problems of a rather specialized spiritual significance is convincingly portrayed, but the average reader may find that the loose structure of the novel has weakened its intended impact. It is interesting to note that it is the last full-length novel to have appeared from the pen of le Fort and that she would now seem to have recognized that the form of the novelle and short story are more suited to her literary talents.

Chapter II

1. Er liebt mich, die ich Gott liebe, also liebt er Gott durch mich. *Schriften* I, p. 428.
2. So hiess es jetzt: um seiner Gottesferne willen darfst du dich niemals von ihm trennen, denn Gott trennt sich ja auch nicht von den Gottesfernen, sondern gerade diese hat Er in Christus gesucht und geliebt. *Schriften* I, pp. 549, 550.
3. Es gibt eine natürliche Haltung, dieser Feindschaft zu begegnen und es gibt eine übernatürliche. Die erste trennt sich von dem Gottlosen, um die eigene Seele zu bewahren, die übernatürliche Haltung harrt an seiner Seite aus. *Schriften* I, p. 623.
4. Veronica's readiness to withhold herself from the sacraments of her Church in order that Enzio's soul might be saved has been the subject of many arguments among Catholic critics of le Fort's work. As these arguments are of a theological rather than of a literary nature, it is not proposed to discuss them here. They have been collected and edited by H. Becher, S.J., in a pamphlet, *Der Kranz der Engel im Widerstreit der Meinungen* (Ehrenwirth Verlag, 1950).
5. Rom ist vorüber, jetzt kommt nur noch Deutschland... Deutschland ist mein Schicksal geworden. *Schriften* I, pp. 343, 345.
6. Grauen vor der metaphysischen Verlassenheit. *Ibid.*, p. 394.
7. Das (Religiöse) spielt doch überhaupt keine Rolle mehr für mich-das ist gar nicht mehr für mich vorhanden. *Ibid.*, p. 362.
8. Die ganz grosse Aufgabe der Zukunkt, ja als sein ganz persönliches Ziel, dieses unfruchtbare Schweifen im Vergangenen aufzugeben und einfach eine neue Wahrheit zu setzen schlicht, fassbar und brauchbar, zu der man sich auch wirklich bekennen, und die man zu leben vermöchte. *Ibid.*, p. 453.
9. Solange sich der Mensch noch von einer höheren Gewalt abhängig weiss, setzt er nicht sein Letztes ein, um dieses wird es bei meinem Werke gehen: es handelt sich um eine unerhörte eigene Kraftentfaltung unseres Volkes, und ich denke nicht daran, sie einschränken zu lassen. *Schriften* I, p. 527.
10. Die nicht mit dem Kriege fertig würden. Er wolle sich mit seinem traurigen Ausgang nicht abfinden, sondern führe ihn in seinem Innern eigenwillig weiter. *Ibid.*, p. 382.
11. Unser Volk von diesem fürchterlichen Frieden zu befreien. *Ibid.*, p. 434.
12. Ausdruck der Reichsherrlichkeit. *Schriften* I, p. 497.
13. Ihm gehe es ja nicht etwa nur um einen Aufstieg unseres Volkes aus der bittersten Not... Was er meine, sei der nie verjährte

Anspruch unseres Volkes, die zeitlose Sendung. . . : die Herrlichkeit des Reiches. *Ibid.*, p. 499.

14. Das Reich ist ewig. . . In meinem Reich wird es kein Sakrament geben. . . Es gibt eben Sieger und Besiegte—von Versöhnung kann im Völkerleben nie die Rede sein. . . Was sollte auch ein Volk mit einem Gott beginnen, vor dem alle Völker Brüder sind. . . In meinem Reiche aber soll es Siegeskrone geben. *Ibid.*, p. 501, 502.

15. Man kann alles, was man will, und was man will, kann man auch. *Schriften* I, p. 396.

16. Cf. Eugen Kogon, Der *S.S. Staat* (Stockholm, 1947). The reader of Kogon's frightening account of the Nazi state will immediately be struck by similarities between his description of the type of attitude which was prevalent in the Nazi state and that portrayed by le Fort in Enzio.

17. For many of the ideas expressed by the professor, le Fort is obviously indebted to her former teacher, Ernst Troeltsch, who was much preoccupied with the role of religion in the preservation of the cultural traditions of Western Europe.

18. Das schopferische Prinzip unserer Kultur, sie war ihr Ursprung und ihre Verheissung, sie war ihre Einheit in der Vielfalt. *Schriften* I, p. 538.

19. Dass der Verrat an der Religion den Verrat an der Kultur nach sich zieht. . . Die abendländische Kultur wird genau so lange leben wie die abendländische Religion lebt. Nicht jene trägt diese, sondern diese jene. *Ibid.*, p. 595.

20. Man kann von einer grossen Abendröte zwar eine Weile leben, aber eben nur noch eine Weile—sie selbst, die Abendröte—kann nicht lange leben, das ist ihrem Wesen nach unmöglich. Wenn sie erscheint, ist die Sonne bereits untergegangen. *Schriften* I, p. 593.

21. Jenseits einer Katastrophe von ungeahntem Ausmass. *Ibid.*, p. 597.

22. Ihn überhaupt nur studierte um ihn zu überwinden. *Schriften* I, p. 519.

23. Die sich nicht wehren können, sondern die ihm (Enzio) verfallen werden rückhaltlos, so wie das blinde Werkzeug der gewissenlosen Hand verfällt. *Ibid.*, p. 566.

24. We use the term *bourgeois* in its ontological sense to designate a spiritual state, a direction of the mind and soul. cf. N. Berdyaev, *The Bourgeois Mind* (London, 1934).

25. Bei ihr ist ja alles nur schöner Anzug. *Schriften* I, p. 391.

26. Ein grosses graues Schiff, still im Mittag verankert. *Schriften* I, p. 143.
27. Wie ein helles hochbemastetes Schiff, das, vor Anker liegend, mit seinem silbernen Kiel das Meer. . . berührte. *Ibid.*, p. 454.
28. Mir war, als müsste ich meine eigene Seele wie ein kleines Licht in die Hand nehmen, damit er an die seine glauben könne. *Ibid.*, p. 149.
29. Dabei war es mir, als trüge ich meine Seele, einem kleinen Licht gleich, in der Hand, denn sein Gesicht erhellte sich jetzt, wie von einem solchen angestrahlt. *Schriften* I, p. 361.
30. Also um mir Licht zu machen bist du hergekommen? *Ibid.*, p. 362.
31. Du stehst da oben in deinem weissen Kleid wie eine Kerze und bei mir ist es schon reichlich dunkel. Willst du nicht herunterkommen und mir etwas leuchten? *Ibid.*, p. 361.
32. Ein magnetischer Strom. *Ibid.*, p. 613.
33. Früher sagten wir immer du seiest ein kleiner Vogel. . . Kannst du auch noch fliegen wie damals? *Schriften* I, pp. 414, 415.
34. Es ging nun langsam mit mir aufwärts. . . so als komme mein Geist aus unermesslichen Fernen zurück, mit gebrochenen Schwingen. *Ibid.*, p. 654.
35. Wie ein Spuk um leere Häuser. *Schriften* I, p. 637.
36. Diese geisterhaften Mondscheinbeleuchtungen einer verwandelten Welt. *Ibid.*, p. 640.

CHAPTER III

The Song at the Scaffold

Having as it were served her literary apprentice-ship with two novels, *The Roman Fountain* (1928) and *The Pope from the Ghetto* (1930), le Fort next turned to the novelle, a form of short story traditionally favored by German writers. *The Song at the Scaffold* (1931)[1] is a masterpiece within this genre and shows le Fort in complete command of both her medium and her material.

The central events of *The Song at the Scaffold* are presented within the framework of a letter written in 1794 by a French nobleman, Herr von Villeroi, to an aristocratic friend of pre-revolutionary days who is now an emigrée. In this letter the writer describes an event he witnessed in Paris during the closing days of the Revolution, the deaths on the scaffold of sixteen Carmelite nuns and that of a young noblewoman, Blanche de la Force. The story of Blanche's life and the events leading up to her death constitute the subject matter of this novelle. Blanche, only child of the free-thinking Marquis de la Force, is presented as an almost pathologically timorous girl. Having been educated by a governess, Madame de Chalais, Blanche, at the age of seventeen, decides to enter the Carmelite convent at Compiègne. She makes this decision partly because she feels a genuine call to the religious life, but partly too because she hopes to find within the convent walls a certain measure of protection from the buffetings of the harsh world. In the convent Blanche learns to come to terms with the strange obsessive fear which has haunted her since birth by accepting it as an integral part of her personality and as a God-given burden. Soon after her arrival at Compiègne, however, a period of trial begins. The revolutionary government orders the dissolution of the religious houses and it becomes gradually more and more apparent that the shadow of the guillotine hangs menacingly over the convent. The nuns greet the prospect of death with characteristic philosophic resignation, and make a solemn pledge to accept such sacrifices as may be demanded of them, even death itself, in order that France may be preserved from a prolongation of the regime of terror. Blanche, however, who fears death above all else, shrinks from making such a vow. She flees from the convent and returns to her home. There further horrors lie in store for her. Her father is murdered by the revolutionaries and they take possession of her home. Blanche, bewildered and dazed, is adopted by them as a sort of mascot and ultimately finds death at their hands.

The genesis of this story is extremely interesting as a revelation of le Fort's attitude to her literary sources and as an example of the interplay of her poetic and creative talents with a philosophical and historical approach to her material. We are fortunate in having in le Fort's own words a description of how this work and its heroine Blanche came to life in her poetic imagination. She writes: "In the strictly historical sense she (Blanche) never really existed, but the very fibres of her tremulous existence had their origins exclusively in my creative imagination. At a period when Germany was a prey to a foreboding of future disasters I conceived this figure as the "incorporation of the fear of dissolution of a moribund age."[2] Initially, therefore, the figure of

Blanche was conceived as mirroring the psychological reaction of the more sensitive of le Fort's intelligent contemporaries to the horror of the Nazi regime and the prevalent sense of impending doom. About this time, while browsing among the archives of Munich University library, le Fort came across a brief account of the heroic death during the French Revolution of sixteen French Carmelites. In a flash of illumination she realized that this episode presented the perfect background for the figure of Blanche which had been haunting her poetic imagination:

> A short note about the Carmelites, singing as they mounted the steps of the scaffold, was responsible for my decision to transpose the figure of Blanche from the present into the period of the French Revolution. In doing this I was acting in accordance with a tendency peculiar to my creative work, namely, to transpose present-day problems and personages to a previous age, so as to be able to shape and form them more objectively and calmly than would be possible if I were hampered by too close a proximity to them.[3]

In this statement we have a clear indication of le Fort's aims and intentions in writing *The Song at the Scaffold*, namely, to give an historical perspective to contemporary problems. Through the story of Blanche questions are posed which are very much to the fore in the consciousness of our times, such as the relevance of divine grace to human action, the reasons for the emergence of evil and its dominion over the minds of men, and the problem of that *insecuritas humana* which often seems to beset the whole of man's life. Le Fort has given depth and perspective to the skeleton story as she found it, and from it has fashioned a positive contribution to the discussion of problems which are relevant to us today.

The main theme of *The Song at the Scaffold* is perhaps

best expressed in the terms of the biblical paradox "My strength finds its full scope in Thy weakness. . . When I am weak, then I am strongest of all" (II Cor. XII, 9.). In effect we may look on the story as an attempt to indicate the effect of grace on human life. An understanding of the Catholic view of grace is fundamental to an appreciation of this story, as it comprises an integral part of le Fort's thought. The workings of divine grace do not conform to human standards. God's grace may intervene when and where man least expects it and may transform the whole pattern of his life. Man has no control over the operation of grace; it stands totally outside the orbit of his volition. Its impact can show up the inadequacy of an existence centered solely on human ideals and the insufficiency of all human endeavor not in consonance with the will of God. It is paradoxical that the most unlikely people are often singled out for the reception of grace; the only prerequisite on the part of the individual is a readiness to surrender the self and to acquiesce completely in the divine will.

The backcloth of the French Revolution, which provides the setting of the story, creates by its very nature an atmosphere of tension. In the pervading disquiet and terror the characters of the story are brought face to face with a personal crisis, and each one must review the basic meaning and purpose of his life. They fall easily into two broad groupings: those who accept the fact that human life has a transcendental aim and purpose and that it is directed by a supernatural force which is superior to man, and those who reject this concept and substitute for it a belief in man's autonomy and self-sufficiency. The two chief protagonists, Blanche and Sister Marie, together with the prioress of the convent, Madame Lidoine, all belong to the first group, but each of them is characterized by her individual attitude and outlook; one might say that they represent three stages of progress in sanctity.

In the heroine of the story, Blanche, le Fort has not only given a subtle analysis of a sensitive character but also a cogent personification of that *Angst* which has haunted the minds of thinking men since Kierkegaard, and is so marked a feature of contemporary living. Perhaps of even greater importance is the specific instance we have here of the impact that divine grace may have on the life of a human being in the most unexpected situation. From her earliest years Blanche is keenly conscious of the impermanence of all temporal phenomena, and is obsessed by an irrational fear and distrust of everything about her. The efforts of her governess to help Blanche overcome her fear by emphasizing the power of Christ the King are successful insofar as they encourage her at least to suppress the outward manifestations of her fear, but they do not succeed in getting down to the root cause and eradicating it. No rational explanation can wholly account for this fear, in itself an essentially irrational phenomenon with no objective basis in reality. It soon becomes obvious to the reader that this fear has its roots neither in the physiological realm nor in the emotional, but that it is conceived basically as a spiritual problem: "It seemed as if this pitiable little life were overshadowed by the expectation of some horrible happening... as if her terrified childish eyes were able to penetrate through the solid framework of her sheltered life to perceive its frightening inherent fragility."[4] After Blanche's entry into the convent at Compiègne various indications are given that she has learned to accept her affliction. Abandoning her former efforts to overcome or to suppress her fear, she now sublimates it to the level of a mystical experience by correlating her suffering with the mental anguish of Christ in Gethsemane, which, significantly, is the name she bears in the religious life. Sister Marie's words alert the reader at this stage to the nature of the change that is taking place in the attitude of the heroine: "Is there not a possibility that fear and horror may be some-

thing deeper than courage, something far more in consonance with the reality of things, that is, with the horrors of
the world?"[5] The mystical experience which Blanche undergoes is at no point overtly elaborated by le Fort, but is
delicately suggested, for as Paul Ernst has said: "one cannot
express in words, which are really thought images, profun-
dities which lie below the margin of conscious thought: one
can only evoke in the reader by certain means the concept
of their existence."[6] Le Fort does this largely by means of
jottings from the notebook of the prioress: "O God, is Your
mercy so great that you pursue a poor soul which cannot rise
above its frailty down to the depths of this very frailty to
unite it at that very level with Your love?"[7] At such points
in the narrative the reader will begin to notice a change
in tone. Although the reader may perceive that Blanche's
attitude toward her fear has changed and that she has undergone what amounts to a mystical experience, the community
at Compiègne has no such insight and the nuns regard
Blanche only as a weak link in the chain that they are forging
for martyrdom. In the eyes of the nuns Blanche's refusal to
join in their pledge to sacrifice their lives in the cause of their
faith and of their country is a clear and unambiguous manifestation of her weakness, and they regard her flight from
the convent immediately prior to the taking of this pledge
as a decided and final expression of her fear. In reality, however, Blanche has not, as they imagine, completely suc-
cumbed to her fear, but her flight signifies her realization of
the fact that it is not the display of heroism, but the willing
acceptance of her weakness which is her appointed role.

After her flight from the convent Blanche is thrown into
the chaos of the Revolution, caught up by the amorphous
mob and enmeshed in its horrible and bloodthirsty toils. She
now moves as one whose mind has been conditioned. "Supped

full with horrors," dazed with fear, her will seems to have become completely paralyzed. The nadir is reached when she drinks of the sacrilegious chalice of blood which the revolutionaries force to her lips. At this point Blanche, in her mystical union with the suffering Christ, is no longer a responsible being, but one whose whole personality has, as it were, been blotted out: "her face was completely devoid of any expression. . . as if it were somehow submerged, no longer there."[8] This symbolic action might be interpreted as the ultimate betrayal of both her class and her faith, but this moment of failure on a human level is selected by le Fort to indicate the operation of divine grace. By the effacement of her personality, by the total suppression of her own ego, Blanche has become an instrument through which the Lord may manifest His power. The final incident of the story cannot be accounted for by psychological motivation, but only by intervention of the supernatural. As Blanche, who has been brought to the Place de la Révolution by her captors to witness the spectacle of the death of the nuns, stands among the onlookers, grace begins to operate within her. The *Veni Creator* is intoned by the nuns as they approach the guillotine one by one, but it gradually diminishes in volume according as the ranks are depleted, until finally its strains are borne by a single voice. As this last voice is silenced in turn, from among the onlookers yet another single voice takes up the hymn. It is that of Blanche, who sings to its conclusion the hymn of her former companions, thus bringing their noble sacrifice to its final consummation. Before she can pronounce the Amen, Blanche is murdered by the enraged mob. Her death, however, is not presented by le Fort as a defeat; at the moment of death she has won a decisive victory over the fear which had haunted her since birth, and has proved herself a worthy bearer of the proud family name, *de la Force*, a name which had for so long appeared as a mockery of her weakness. Blanche has, in her last moments, asserted her personality in what for le Fort is the highest manner possible; she has become a vehicle for the operation of grace, a martyr in the fullest sense of the word. For the narrator of the story, who witnessed the scene, the deaths of Blanche and the nuns have a special significance in that for him they herald the return to normality and the ending of mob rule: "This song seemed to transcend its temporal environment, it transcended space; it effaced the concept of chaos; I suddenly had the feeling I was among men again."[9] A few days later his premonitions are proved to have been correct, and the Revolution ends.

The use of symbolism is an integral part of this novelle and the role of the mob has a particular symbolic significance as the personification of the forces of chaos. The mob plays an important role in Blanche's life. Her birth coincides with the first outbreak of mob violence and her life ends with the termination of its most sanguinary excesses. To the attack on her mother's coach by the *sansculottes* shortly before her birth may be attributed that unusual fear and shrinking from life which are Blanche's outstanding characteristics. The terrifying refrains of the songs of the mob, the *Carmagnole* and the *Ca ira*, constantly disturb the quiet and peace she seeks in the convent. Blanche's last prayer, as she joins in the beautiful liturgical hymn of the community as they advance to their death, is an invocation to the Holy Spirit to enlighten the deluded and perverted minds of her persecutors. The symbolic role of the mob in her life is underlined by the fact that Blanche, unlike her companions, does not meet death at the guillotine, but at the hands of the infuriated revolutionaries. The use of the family name is also not without symbolic significance. This scion of a noble house with its challenging title *de la Force* is, from a human point of view, characterized above all by a craven weakness, but once informed by grace, this weakness is transformed into strength which transcends even the terrors of death.

In Blanche le Fort has shown the operation of grace in a weak character: in Sister Marie de l'Incarnation she also shows the operation of grace, but in a very different context. To Blanche grace imparts the courage to face death fearlessly; to Marie it gives the strength to face life, and to renounce the martyr's death to which she had always aspired.

Marie, illegitimate daughter of a noble house of France, has entered the convent at Compiègne with a specific purpose in view, namely, "to atone for the sinful pleasures of the Court, of which her own life was the fruit."[10] Her background is highly relevant to her character and attitude, determining, as it does, the whole aim of her life as a nun. The distinguishing feature of Marie's character is her courage. To Marie the martyr's death so feared by Blanche is not something inspiring dread, but, on the contrary, she sees in it the ideal culmination of her life in the convent. But to le Fort, the flaw in Marie's character is to be found in this desire for a martyr's death, the purpose of which she herself determines in advance. She wishes her death to be a sacrifice which may avert the impending chaos, the means of saving her faith and her country: "The sooner this world makes us feel its hatred, the better for the world."[11] This desire, although good in itself, yet falls short of the perfection demanded of the true martyr, for, to quote T. S. Eliot, "a martyrdom is never the design of man... The martyr no longer desires anything for himself, not even the glory of martyrdom."[12] Marie's weakness lies in the fact that she "has not lost her will in the will of God,"[13] as the true martyr must do. In leading the nuns to pledge their lives for their country Marie is asserting her own will; she is succumbing to Thomas à Becket's greatest temptation: "to do the right deed for the wrong reason."[14] In the course of the novelle, Marie's readiness to die has evolved into a positive desire for death; her anticipation of her fate has changed "from an attitude of resignation to an expressed longing for death."[15] After taking the vow, the desire for a sacrificial death becomes the dominating factor in Marie's life, and from this point onwards her only fear is "not the fear of the sacrifice, but rather the fear that she might be prevented from making this sacrifice."[16] The paradoxical situation is that whereas the source of Blanche's final strength is ultimately to be found in her weakness, in Marie's case the converse holds true; the root of her weakness lies in her strength.

In the course of the narrative Marie's character undergoes a development. Absent by chance from Compiègne when the nuns of the convent are arrested, Marie, "who had been the inspiring figure in animating all the others to be ready for sacrifice, sees herself excluded from the sacrificial act."[17] In her acquiescent acceptance of this disappointment she evinces her greatness of character. Although present in Paris as the nuns mount the steps of the scaffold to their death, she does nothing which would imperil her own safety and enable her to join them in death. It is by this willing renunciation of the martyr's crown that Marie reaches the stature attained by Blanche in accepting it. She, "for whom it is harder to live than to die,"[18] makes thus what is for her the greatest sacrifice of all. Her final sacrifice is enhanced by the oblivion which surrounds it; she knows that her name, unlike those of her companions, will be unsung by posterity. Significantly, Marie's last message to the prioress, indicative of the change in her attitude, is fated never to reach its destination "and so the sacrifice of Marie de l'Incarnation ends, enshrouded in silence."[19]

In le Fort's interpretation of the fates of Blanche and Marie the normal human values are strangely reversed. Blanche, initially so weak and in no sense of the word heroic, dies a courageous martyr's death; Marie, of whom it is said that "from a human point of view she, more so than any of the others, seemed to have been cut out for martyrdom," [20] is denied the fulfillment of her wish. In the view of le Fort, each of these characters has attained full spiritual stature by accepting her particular destiny; Blanche by dying, Marie by living on. Each has finally subjected her will to a higher power, and by so doing has enabled divine grace to operate within her.

The mean between Blanche's abject fear of death and Marie's ardent desire for it is represented by the prioress, Madame Lidoine. Her words reflect the truly Christian attitude to martyrdom: "What is really important is not that we should realize our own ambitions, however exalted these may be, but that God's purpose may be fulfilled."[21] Madame Lidoine neither fears martyrdom excessively, nor does she seek it out, but she shows herself willing to be the instrument through which God may carry out His designs.

Blanche's father, the Marquis de la Force, a lightly sketched character, represents the point of view of those who reject the concept of a supernatural basis to life. He plays no vital part in the action, but his ideas and attitudes are not without importance for an understanding of the historical background. The Marquis de la Force is a follower of the Encyclopedists, an admirer of Diderot and of Voltaire. He believes that all natural phenomena are, and must be, explicable on rational grounds. Thus, although his daughter's excessive timidity puzzles him a little, he rationalizes its origins by attributing it to prenatal influences—to his wife's terrifying experiences when her carriage was attacked by the mob at the wedding celebrations of Louis XVI and to Blanche's premature birth soon afterwards. "Poor timorous child, it is clear that the unfortunate circumstances of her birth have determined her whole attitude to life."[22] The Marquis is a man of high ideals who believes in the innate nobility of man, and fondly pins his faith on what he regards as the impregnable bastion of eighteenth-century culture. His high-minded ideals nonetheless prove inadequate to meet the turbulence of his age, and the weakness in his philosophy of life becomes apparent as the crisis develops. Throughout his life the Marquis has ignored those aspects of reality which ran counter to his philosophy, but the Revolution compels him to take cognizance of them. As the shibboleths of the rationalists—which they had never really thought out to their logical conclusion—are taken over by the mob and are translated into acts of violence, he must face the fact that "even the forces of chaos are part of nature. . . even the beast in man."[23] As the Marquis' world collapses at its foundations, he sees that his faith in man, in culture and civilization has been misplaced. To his ultimate fate but slight importance is assigned; he is just another victim of the Revolution.

The ideals of Blanche's governess, Madame de Chalais, like those of the Marquis, are shown as equally inadequate to withstand the test of the Revolution. Although she is superficially pious, Madame de Chalais bases her faith on criteria which are basically temporal. Her religion is one-sided; it is based on the principle of cause and effect. She is convinced that justice will be meted out in this world, that the good will be rewarded and that the wicked will suffer for their crimes, and she elects to overlook any experience which would run counter to this belief. Her attitude toward unpleasant truth is symbolized in her tight-fitting bodice, which is her armor against the harsh realities of the world: "She had a great facility in avoiding awkward questions. Blanche occasionally had the impression that such questions rebounded from the whalebones of her tight-fitting bodice."[24] When reality suddenly and brutally impinges on the world of Madame de Chalais as the Revolution gains momentum, her armor is no proof against it. The whole fabric of her piety is rent: "It was as if all her piety had suddenly abandoned her."[25] This collapse is indicated symbolically by le Fort: "Her tight bodice was torn, the broken whalebones protruding pitiably from the torn silk."[26] Madame de Chalais' end, like that of the Marquis, is not described in detail, but a terse statement indicates that her physical death occurs within a few days of the collapse of her spiritual world. Through the Marquis and Madame de Chalais le Fort shows up the inherent weakness of a purely rationalistic and pragmatic philosophy, a weakness which she highlights by throwing it into contrast with the strength, derived from faith, of the main characters.

The epistolary form adopted for the story permits and justifies the introduction of a commentary on the events by two contemporary figures not directly implicated in the action. The views of the writer of the letter, Herr von Villeroi, are neatly juxtaposed to those of its recipient, who is addressed as a disciple of Rousseau. She, like the Marquis and Madame de Chalais, is portrayed as a believer in man's innate nobility and goodness, and in the dignified manner in which so many French noblemen faced death she sees her beliefs sustained. To her their equanimity is a forceful and meaningful indication of "the dignity of human nature confronting the stormy seas of terrifying chaos."[27] Prior to the Revolution her philosophy of reason had been shared by the letter writer; he too had believed in the invincible nature of his civilization and culture. But the scenes he witnessed in Paris, in which both great courage and horrible violence were displayed, have aroused fundamental questions in the mind of Herr von Villeroi. In the course of the letter he seeks to penetrate beneath the external manifestations of what he has seen. He cannot bring himself to accept the fact that the atrocities committed by the mob are explicable solely as a consequence of the social injustice endured by the mass of the people. Gradually he comes to see them as a surfacing of mysterious forces latent in humanity. Similarly, the dignified deaths of the noblemen are not to him primarily an expression of the nobility of human nature but rather a pathetic, but courageous, token of resistance, "the final brave rally of a disintegrating culture."[28] The two contrasting interpretations of events are highlighted *à propos* of Blanche's death: to the lady it is a supreme expression of human courage, but to Herr von Villeroi, who is conversant with the episodes which preceded it, it is a manifestation of the power of the supernatural and a visible indication of the workings of divine grace. It is evident that in *The Song at the Scaffold* le Fort has made skillful use of the device of setting the main story within the framework of a letter. By means of this technique the intensity and urgency of the central story reach the reader at one remove via the account of the letter writer, making possible an unbiased factual account of events, since the writer is not personally involved in them. Yet at no point does his letter become a mere documentary report. Its general conversational tone, together with the writer's concern to impress on his friend the change of mind effected in him by the events he describes, ensures that the reader's attention is actively engaged and that he becomes implicated in the issues raised by the narrative.

The problems treated in this novelle have a particular relevance to our times. The theme of the impact of grace on man's life is one that is very much to the fore in the literary consciousness of the twentieth century, and in this connection it would be interesting to compare le Fort's treatment with that of writers like Werner Bergengruen or Graham Greene. Le Fort's approach is always unambiguous, and one of the outstanding features of *The Song at the Scaffold* is the clarity with which the main themes and their relevance beyond the immediate context of the story impinge on the reader. The *Angst* which le Fort depicts as pervading prerevolutionary France is not merely to be interpreted as a fear of the impending catastrophe; it is the fundamental *insecuritas humana*, it is that basic fear that existentialist philosophy would claim to be the distinguishing mark of fallen man. At moments of unrest or crisis man seems unable to control this fear, which, once liberated, finds its expression in deeds of violence. In human terms the expression of what le Fort designates "these forces of chaos which always lie dormant below the surface of things visible"[29] is the mob. As part of a mob the individual becomes completely submerged; his personality is eclipsed, and under the sway of mob rule he can no longer be regarded as a responsible human being. Man is usually powerless to overcome the forces of evil and chaos rampant in the world that are personified in the mob, but le Fort wishes to show, here that real victory over them cannot be assessed by ordinary human standards alone. Le Fort's interpretation of the French Revolution, not as a simple revolt against economic and social injustice, but as a phenomenon of more far-reaching importance is also not without significance for us today: "Abuses and faults in the economic system can only partially be regarded as the causes of revolutions; they rather trigger off the explosions. In their ultimate analysis revolutions are the eruption of the fear of dissolution of a moribund age."[30] It hardly needs emphasis that such outbreaks of violence as were witnessed in the eighteenth century are not peculiar to past ages; indeed, the accuracy of le Fort's assessment of the problems in this novelle has become horrifyingly obvious since the book appeared in 1931.

Le Fort's approach to the problems she raises in *The Song at the Scaffold* is basically determined by her religious beliefs; she cannot, however, be said in any way to force her views on the reader. She makes no attempt to suppress or minimize the possible rational explanation of the events she describes, nor does she attempt to obscure our judgment by appeals to our emotions. By allowing the writer and the recipient of the letter to hold divergent interpretations of the story of Blanche, she makes the reader take sides with one or other of them; perhaps the most flattering appeal to the intelligent reader is the concluding phrase of the story: *Tua res agitur*.

The popularity and appeal of *The Song at the Scaffold* may be gauged by the many translations of the work that have appeared and also by the variety of media for which it has been adapted. The French writer Georges Bernanos used it as a basis for his *Dialogues des Carmélites*, and his version in turn was adapted by Poulenc as the libretto for his opera *Les Carmélites*. It has also been adapted as a radio play, and a film version of it appeared in 1960. Since these various adaptations have all helped to make le Fort's work more widely known, it is perhaps relevant to touch on the relation of some of them to their original. Shortly after the end of the last war a French film company approached le Fort for permission to make a film based on her novelle, for which Georges Bernanos was to write the dialogue. For some years nothing was heard of the project, until Albert Béguin, Bernanos' literary executor (the latter had died in 1948), produced the manuscript of the play we now know as *Les Dialogues des Carmélites*.[31] It would seem clear that this text could never have been intended as the script for a film, since it does not exploit any of the cinematic possibilities of the plot or seem otherwise suitable for the screen. It can stand perfectly well alone as a dramatic unit for stage production, and it is as such that it has enjoyed great success in the course of the past few years. It seems important to emphasize that Bernanos has slightly altered le Fort's approach to the theme of the story. Both the novelle and the play treat of the theme of grace and the victory of the supernatural, but the angle of approach is slightly different in each case. In le Fort's work the heroine receives the courage and grace for her final sacrifice directly from God; in the play the dying prioress is used as an intermediary as, on her deathbed, she passes on her own strength to the weak novice. This shift in emphasis amounts to a slight distortion of le Fort's main idea, as she herself has pointed out.[32] Both Poulenc's operatic version and the film, *Les Carmélites*, follow Bernanos and suggest the importance of vicarious suffering in the operation of divine grace, and for this reason it is important to bear in mind that le Fort's primary concern was with the direct intervention of the supernatural. Apart from this, the other alterations are largely dictated by the demands of the different genres, and by and large they have remained faithful to the original.

In using the form of the novelle to give literary expression to a facet of experience outside the realm of normal tangible reality, Gertrud von le Fort is following in the German tradition established by Goethe and Kleist. "The novelle," writes E. K. Bennett in his *History of the German Novelle*, "is in its very nature concerned with the irrational elements in life,"[33] and in it man "appears as a being whose fate is determined by the impact of an external event."[34] *The Song at the Scaffold* has all the characteristic features of the good novelle. The external event whose impact has a determining effect on the lives of the characters is, of course, the French Revolution, and in this event we have also, as indicated above, an eruption of "the irrational forces in life." From a structural point of view *The Song at the Scaffold* is characterized by brevity, unity and concentration. These qualities highlight the central theme with its relevance to the modern world and they combine with its intellectual and emotional appeal to make it a masterpiece in miniature.

CHAPTER III

1. English translation, *The Song at the Scaffold* (London, 1953; United States, Henry Holt & Co., 1933).
2. Sie hat im historischen Sinn niemals gelebt, sondern sie empfing den Atem ihres zitternden Daseins ausschliesslich aus meinem eigenen Innern. . . Geboren aus dem tiefen Grauen einer Zeit, die in Deutschland überschattet wurde von den vorauseilenden Ahnungen kommender Geschicke, stieg diese Gestalt vor mir auf gleichsam als die Verkörperung der Todesangst einer zu Ende gehenden Epoche. "Zu Georges Bernanos' *Die begnadete Angst*," *Aufzeichnungen*, p. 83.
3. Eine kleine Notiz über die singend zum Schafott ziehenden Karmeliterinnen löste den Entschluss aus, den Schauplatz für des Auftreten meiner kleinen Blanche aus der Gegenwart in die französische Revolution zu verlegen. Ich folgte damit einer meiner Dichtung auch sonst naheliegenden Neigung, aktuelle Probleme und Gestalten in die Vergangenheit zurückzuspiegeln, um sie, von der allzu bedrängenden Nähe gelöst, reiner und ruhiger formen zu können. "Zu Georges Bernanos' Die begnadete Angst," *Aufzeichnungen*, pp. 83, 84.
4. Es war, als schwebe dieses bedauernswerte kleine Leben in der beständigen Erwartung irgendeines grauenvollen Ereignisses. . . oder als reiche sein grosser, erschrockener Kinderblick durch das feste Gefüge des gesicherten Daseins überall in eine entsetzliche Zerbrechlichkeit hinab. *Schriften* I, p. 15.
5. Besteht nicht die Möglichkeit, dass sie (Furcht und Schauder) etwas viel Tieferes sein können als Mut, etwas, das weit mehr der Wirklichkeit der Dinge, das heisst, den Schrecken der Welt entspricht. *Ibid.,* p. 27.
6. (Man kann) solche Tiefen, da sie eben unter dem Gedanklichen liegen, auch nicht durch die Gedankenbilder, nämlich die Worte ausdrücken; man kann nur durch gewisse Mittel im Leser die Vorstellung erwecken, dass sie da seien. *Der Weg zur Form,* 1928, p. 95.
7. O Gott. . . Ist Deine Barmherzigkeit so gross, dass Du einer armen Seele, die ihre Schwachheit nicht zu überwinden vermag, bis eben in diese Schwachheit hinab folgst, um sie gerade dort mit Deiner Liebe zu vereinen? *Schriften* III, p. 52.

8. Ihr Gesicht war vollkommen ausdruckslos, gleichsam in sich selbst untergesunken—nicht mehr da. *Schriften* III, p. 71, 72.
9. Dieser Gesang hob das Zeitgefühl vollkommen auf—er hob auch den Raum auf— . . er hob die Vorstellung des Chaos auf; ich hatte plötzlich wieder das Gefühl: ich war unter Menschen! *Schriften* III, p. 87.
10. Die Sünden des Hofes, denen sie die Entstehung ihres Lebens verdankte. . . zu sühnen. *Schriften* III, p. 26.
11. Je eher die Welt uns ihren Hass fühlen lässt, um so besser für diese Welt. *Schriften* III, p. 44.
12. T. S. Eliot, *Murder in the Cathedral* (London, 1935), p. 49.
13. *Ibid.*, p. 44.
14. *Ibid.*, p. 49.
15. Von der Haltung der blossen Bereitschaft zum offenen Wunsch. *Schriften* III, p. 45.
16. Nicht die Furcht des Opfers—es war die Furcht, an ihrem eigenen Opfer verhindert zu werden. *Ibid.*, p. 64.
17. Welche die Seele des Opferwillens aller gewesen war, sah sich vom Opfer ausgeschlossen. *Ibid.*, p. 80.
18. Leben ist schwerer als Sterben. *Schriften* III, p. 81.
19. Und so endet. . . das Opfer der Marie de l'Incarnation in tiefem Schweigen. *Ibid.*, p. 83.
20. Von den Menschen aus war gerade ihr vor allen anderen das Martyrium zugedacht. *Ibid.*, p. 82.
21. Denn nicht darauf kommt es an, dass wir unsere eigenen Ziele, und wären es die erhabensten, verwirklichen, sondern dass diejenigen Gottes verwirklicht werden. *Schriften* III, p. 46.
22. Armes, ängstliches Kind, die traurigen Umstände seiner Geburt bestimmen offenbar seine ganze Haltung zum Leben. *Ibid.*, p. 11.
23. Auch das Chaos ist Natur, auch die Bestie im Menschen. *Schriften* III, p. 10.
24. Sie besass eine grosse Fähigkeit im Abschieben unbequemer Fragen; Blanche hatte zuweilen die Vorstellung, als prallten sie an den Fischbeinstäben ihres etwas zu engen Mieders ab. *Schriften* III, p. 18.
25. Es war, als ob all ihre Frömmigkeit plötzlich ein Ende gefunden habe. *Ibid.*, p. 62.
26. Ihr enges Mieder stand offen: die Fischbeinstäbe waren. . . zerbrochen und spiessten jämmerlich aus der zerknitterten Seide hervor. *Ibid.*, p. 62.
27. Die Würde der menschlichen Natur gegenüber den Wogen eines grauenvollen Chaos. *Schriften* III, p. 9.
28. Das letzte Aufgebot einer zusammenbrechenden Kuetur. *Schriften* III, p. 10.

29. Das ewig im Untergrund der Dinge schlummernde Chaos. *Schriften* III, p. 13.
30. Revolutionen werden ja immer nur bedingt durch Misswirtschaft und Fehler des Systems verursacht, diese lösen sie vielmehr nur aus: ihr eigentliches Wesen ist der Ausbruch der Todesangst einer zu Ende gehenden Epoche. *Schriften* III, p. 12.
31. The relation of Bernanos' play to le Fort's novelle is discussed in detail in S. Meredith Murray's excellent study, *La Genèse de "Dialogues des Carmélites"* (Paris, 1963).
32. "Zu Georges Bernanos, *Die begnadete Angst*," *Aufzeichnungen,* p. 82.
33. E. K. Bennett, *History of the German Novelle* (London, 1934), p. 49.
34. *Ibid.*

CHAPTER IV

The Wedding at Magdeburg

The theme of *The Wedding at Magdeburg* (1938), like that of *The Roman Fountain*, is one that has very obvious connections with le Fort's background and experience. As a descendant of French Huguenots who fled their fatherland in face of religious persecution, le Fort was always interested in confessional problems, and her studies of history and theology strengthened this interest. Her conversion to Catholicism in 1926 resolved many personal problems, but it also made her more acutely aware of wider issues, above all of the tragedy of the cleavage between Christians of various denominations. One of her major experiences as a convert, she tells us, was "the realization that the Great Schism was less a religious schism than a sundering of the bonds of charity and love, and if theologians are not animated by this all-embracing *caritas*, their efforts to restore the lost unity of Christendom are foredoomed to failure."[1] This quotation shows how le Fort anticipates some of the ecumenical problems of our time, and how she stresses the basic prerequisite for their solution. The narrative *The Wedding at Magdeburg* presents a perfect setting for the further formulation and expansion of her views.

The historical background and perspective of the story are

provided by the Thirty Years War, a war which brought about the final disintegration of the Holy Roman Empire of the German people and marked the disappearance of a united Christendom, which, with its background of a unified faith, had constituted such an integral part of the unity of the Reich. The starting point of the narrative is the period immediately following on the promulgation of the Edict of Restitution by the Habsburg Emperor Ferdinand on March 16, 1629. The threat to enforce this edict provoked a violent upsurge of feeling against the Kaiser on the part of the Protestant citizens of Magdeburg. There were even those who wished to resist its implementation by recourse to arms. The narrative covers the initial period of indecision, the revolt of the burghers, and culminates in the victory of the Imperial troops and the sacking of the town.

To arrive at a true picture of the events leading to this disaster, le Fort made a profound preliminary study of all available sources, and she handles her material with a meticulous regard for historical accuracy. It is most likely that her primary source was a contemporary account of the siege by one Otto Guericke, sometime Mayor of Madgeburg.[2] From this account it can be seen that her depiction of the actions of the main characters and their problems is historically accurate, and that only the women who figure in the novel are fictitious.

While the events chronicled are, in their broad outline, historically accurate, le Fort's interpretation of them is characteristic and personal. She underlines throughout the necessity for tolerance and understanding among Christians of all denominations, and stresses the line of demarcation which must be drawn between religion, in essence something spiritual, and politics, which pertains to an exclusively secular sphere. Arising from her treatment of these two problems, a number of subsidiary problems arise. Foremost among these are the danger inherent in political power and the threat which it may constitute to individual liberty of conscience, the important role of woman as preserver and transmitter of the basic human values, and the disaster which may accrue when pride and self-interest are allowed to dominate man's actions.

All these themes are, however, subsidiary to the main theme, the importance of the virtue of *caritas*—Christian love in its widest connotation—as man's lodestar and the guiding principle of his actions. Le Fort presents the lack of this virtue in the victors of Magdeburg as a factor which nullified material success. In the sacking of the town she sees the collapse of the last hope for restoration of unity in Western Christendom. Personal ambitions should, in her view, have been subordinated to the interests of the larger and more far-reaching issues of the day. By presenting these historical events in the perspective of world history and by interpreting their significance in the light of her own philosophy of life the author has imprinted on the narrative an individual and unique stamp. The solution she offers is as applicable to the world today as to seventeenth-century Germany.

To illustrate her themes Gertrud von le Fort chooses an allegorical form, and in the title, *The Wedding at Magdeburg*, we have the key to the allegory. In broad outline we have here the story of a courtship and marriage, worked out simultaneously on two carefully coordinated levels. The basis for the allegory was provided by the contemporary identification of the city of Magdeburg with the maiden depicted on its coat of arms. C. V. Wedgwood in her *History of the Thirty Years War* tells us that

> the old Wendish name of the great episcopal town Magataburg had been slurred into the popular German form which meant virgin city, and the accidental corruption had acquired in the last century a romantic significance

from the prolonged resistance of the burghers to the attacks of Charles V. . . . Over the chief gate was the statue of a young girl with a virgin's wreath in her hand and the device "Who will take it?"[3]

Contemporary songs and broadsheets, which compared the battle for the city with a courtship by two rivals and adjured the maiden city to withstand the elderly wooer (the Kaiser) and to await her liberation by the younger suitor (the Swedish king), have also been made use of by le Fort, who fully exploits the potential of the ready-made allegory she found at her disposal. She has skillfully linked the fate of the city with that of her heroine, Erdmuth Plögen. In Erdmuth, who is unfaithful to her betrothed, Willigis Ahlemann, and who admits to her chamber "the false bridegroom" (der falsche Bräutigam), the Swede, Falkenberg, the fate of the city of Magdeburg is allegorically portrayed. Falkenberg, the "false bridegroom" admitted by both Erdmuth and the city, draws together the two levels of the story, the real and the allegorical. The action of the novel is divided into three stages, corresponding to the three traditional ceremonial stages of the wedding celebration; these three stages are related both to the maiden Erdmuth and to the maiden city. A brief résumé of the outline of these three sections will illustrate how le Fort has coordinated the two levels of the narrative.

The Kaiser's decision to enforce the Edict of Restitution on the city of Magdeburg by force of arms sets the action in motion. He has ordered General Tilly to lay siege to the city and the latter has taken up his headquarters in the nearby town of Hameln. As a countermove the Swedes offer the citizens of Magdeburg military aid to withstand the expected siege. The town councillors are reluctant to make a final choice in the dilemma confronting them, and in this explosive situation the action of the novel begins.

The first section, *der Jungfrauenabend* (the pre-nuptial celebrations), opens in the cathedral in Magdeburg where the Protestant Pastor Bake is exhorting his congregation to enter into an alliance with the Swedish king against the Kaiser. Seated in the church awaiting the publication of their marriage banns are Erdmuth Plögen and Willigis Ahlemann. Before the pastor's sermon ends, Willigis, fearing that the exhortation may result in immediate action on the part of the townspeople, rushes out without a word of explanation to his bride. The events of that evening and Willigis' failure to appear at the *Jungfrauenabend* are of great moment both for Erdmuth and for the city. The two levels on which the narrative runs are correlated for the reader by the comment: "It may well be that this will prove to be the last evening on which Magdeburg also can claim to be inviolate."[4] The action next moves to the City Hall where the Swedish ambassador is explaining the position to the town councillors. His speech makes them realize with dismay that the strong strategic position of their city constitutes a great potential danger. Up to this point they had considered Magdeburg only as the "key to everything."[5] Now it is revealed to them in a new light as "completely checkmated on the chessboard between the two opposing armies."[6] This section ends with the admission of the Swedish commander, Falkenberg, to the town and his meeting with Erdmuth Plögen, who, believing herself deserted by her fiancé, Willigis, leads him to the City Hall.

The second section, *der Ehrentanz* (the dance of honor), opens in the Imperial camp at Hameln, where Willigis has ridden to appeal to General Tilly to intervene and forestall disaster by getting the Edict revoked. Having been made to realize the full gravity of the situation, Tilly agrees to send his Jesuit aide to Vienna with the request that the implementation of the Edict be postponed for forty years. On his return to Magdeburg, Willigis, who has been branded a traitor by his fellow citizens, is refused admission to the town. However, forcing his way past the guard at the city gate, he rushes to the City Hall, there to be confronted with the spectacle of his fiancée, Erdmuth, dancing the *Ehrentanz*—the prerogative of the prospective bridegroom—with Falkenberg. This action on the part of Erdmuth is a token of her acceptance of the "false bridegroom"; it also symbolizes the city's acceptance of the alliance with the Swedish king.

The third section, *Das Brautgemach* (the marriage chamber) deals with the final stages of the wooing of both Erdmuth and of the city. In this section the futile efforts to avert the catastrophe of those who were able to foresee both the material and spiritual disasters which the sack of the city would bring in its train are developed. It is, however, in vain that Erdmuth and Magdeburg await the arrival of the promised rescuer, and both are fated to become victims of the rapacious lust of the soldiery.

Before the action proper is finally engaged, the issues involved for the various parties are laid before the reader at some length. The dilemma is first seen through the eyes of the town councillors who find themselves in a situation in which their loyalties to their faith and to their Kaiser have become mutually exclusive. Staunchly Protestant, they are adamant in their resolve to withstand any attempt to enforce the Edict of Restitution which would compel them to relinquish their cathedral and would bring them under Catholic jurisdiction. Yet they also owe allegiance to the Reich, and a military alliance with any foreign potentate is consequently tantamount to treason to the Reich. The only answer they see to the problem is in a confirmation of the city's previous status as a "free city of the Reich." As such they would not be subject to the Treaty of Augsburg and to its ruling '*Cujus regio, ejus religio*"; they would be outside the jurisdiction of the Kaiser, who would be powerless to enforce the Edict. Ferdinand's refusal to confirm this old status, however, confronts the council with the alternative of a betrayal of either their faith or of their Kaiser. The problem is next presented from the point of view of the loyalist Imperialist party. Here too, in the attempt to find a solution to the difficulty by using military force to resolve what was fundamentally a spiritual problem, there is evidence of confused thinking. The sole concern of the generals Pappenheim and Mansfeld is war, with its excitement and triumphs; its real issues lie beyond the range of both their comprehension and their interest. To them the whole problem is unequivocal: "If the Magdeburg town council really wishes to preserve its loyalty to the Kaiser, it must return to the Kaiser's religion."[7] Thus le Fort presents the views of the two opposing groups. For a more detailed analysis of the problem let us turn to the individual characters.

The two chief characters of the novel, Willigis Ahlemann, a Protestant citizen of Magdeburg, and General Tilly, commander of the Catholic Imperial army, may be regarded as the more enlightened representatives of their respective creeds. Each meets with a total lack of comprehension from his associates, represented respectively by the town councillors and by the generals.

Willigis Ahlemann is presented as "a fine fellow, full of good will, with a mind attuned to the great scheme of things."[8] This ability to see things in their proper perspective, in a context wider than the purely personal, distinguishes Willigis from his fellow Magdeburgers. His discussion with General Tilly at Hameln forms the nexus of the argument of the novel. Willigis paints a clear picture of Magdeburg's position should the Kaiser insist on enforcing the Edict: "If His Imperial Majesty does not withdraw the Edict, no Protestant can remain a loyal subject of the Emperor."[9] In this statement the root of the problem is couched. The Kaiser's decision to have recourse to force of arms in this instance is inherently wrong; it is in effect the arrogation to himself of a right he does not possess. The patent sincerity of Willigis and his conviction that "It is impossible that the Empire and the Faith should issue two contradictory commands. . . Faith is a matter exclusively concerned with God,"[10] soon convince Tilly of a truth which he had previousy apprehended intuitively, if not intellectually.

Whereas Willigis has little difficulty in impressing his convictions on General Tilly and in bringing him round to his point of view, his efforts to get the town councillors of Magdeburg to capitulate to the Imperial army and thus save the city meet with failure. He cannot make them see that an alliance with the Swedes will not ameliorate their position. In theory they accept his proposition that "what an individual believes is not the business of His Imperial Majesty, but God's business,"[11] but they fail to put this belief into practice when they turn to Gustav Adolf for military aid to protect their religious interests. All Willigis' efforts to avert this alliance are to no avail, and in despair he must abandon his townspeople to their inevitable doom. Although Willigis' mission as an intermediary fails, his inherent strength of character enables him to rise superior to the tragic fate which befalls his native city and his fiancée. He succumbs only temporarily to wounded pride at having been deserted by Erdmuth and finally vindicates the power of genuine Christian love and the truth of the motto emblazoned above the patrician Plögen door, "Love is as powerful as death,"[12] by making the faithless and unhappy Erdmuth his bride.

While Willigis accepts a compromise in his personal affairs that may give him a modicum of happiness, the life of his Catholic counterpart, Tilly, is destined to end on a tragic note. Tilly's dilemma is the clash between his personal con-

victions and beliefs and his obligations and duty as supreme
commander of the Kaiser's army. Willigis' arguments have
shaken his belief in the purpose and justice of the war in
which he is engaged, and his tragedy may be said to begin
when he understands that it is no longer possible to realize
the great ambition of his life—the restoration of a united
Christendom under a Catholic *aegis*. After this interview
with Willigis he tries to save the situation by sending a plea
to the Kaiser to postpone the implementation of the Edict.
With the refusal of the Kaiser to accede to this request, Tilly's tragic conflict, the dichotomy between his personal conviction and his duty as commander of the army, becomes
acute. The delaying tactics in which he now engages can,
however, only postpone the inevitable. When the Swedish
army advances to aid the besieged city, Tilly's hand is forced
by military strategy and he orders the attack on the city. His
duty as a soldier must now, he feels, take precedence over
all other considerations, emotional and moral: "All I really
know is that I am a soldier; a soldier's duty is to obey the
Ratio belli."[13] The decision to storm the city marks the climax of Tilly's mental crisis, and as the solution of the tragic
dilemma grows increasingly more difficult, his physical appearance begins to reflect his interior struggle: "His Excellency looked as if he were standing alone among leafless trees,
with an autumnal light focused on him."[14] A final note of
tragic irony is struck by Tilly's realization that posterity will
regard him as a fanatical zealot and will ascribe to him full
responsibility for the massacre at Magdeburg which he had
tried so desperately to prevent: "Your Excellency will be
branded as a sinister religious fanatic. The good name of
Your Catholic Excellency will be besmirched. Your Excellency will be held responsible for crimes which you never
committed."[15] By making no attempt to exonerate himself
or to minimize his responsibility for the catastrophe, Tilly

demonstrates the basic qualities of his character, the virtues of self-abnegation and submissive acceptance of fate.

One aspect of the portrait of Tilly which gives expression to an important facet of the theme of the novel is one which may not find ready acceptance with the average reader, namely, his almost mystical relation with his banner. This is nonetheless important, and it is not without significance that le Fort stresses that "Mary did not achieve victory with a sword in her hand, but by a sword transfixing her heart. Her victory was through the suffering love of her Divine Son."[16] Tilly, as he stands among the ruins of Magdeburg, is able to apply this paradox to his own situation and he can finally assert with conviction: "In the midst of defeat... there is victory."[17]

The pre-eminently Christian qualities of Willigis and the mystical views of Tilly are not shared by the two clerical representatives in the novel, who are schematically the foils of Willigis and Tilly and are depicted as belonging to a lower plane in the hierarchy of spiritual values. Both Pastor Bake and the Jesuit play the role of representatives of the Church militant; they typify that short-sighted fanaticism so typical of wartime mentality then as now, a fanaticism which rendered nugatory the approach of more reasonable men. Both are fundamentally good men, who are motivated neither by personal greed nor by ambition, but rather by an over-zealous desire to see their espoused cause victorious. In the course of the novel both of them come to realize that in their negotiations to further the victory of their respective causes they have been unmindful of the basic precept of *caritas*. The course of events culminating in the downfall of the city brings both of them to a re-appraisal of their attitudes, and they come to see that the authenticity of spiritual truths cannot be measured in terms of temporal success. It is the tragic fate of both Pastor Bake and the Jesuit to witness their own mistaken zeal precipitating the downfall of the cause they champion.

The parallel between the roles of Pastor Bake and the Jesuit is not quite exact and mathematical. Of the two the Jesuit is the more straightforward character. To him the issue is unequivocal: the rebellious citizens of Magdeburg are heretics who constitute a serious threat to the unity of the Church, and secondarily, to the unity of the Reich, and as such they must at all costs be suppressed. This opinionated, self-righteous young priest regards Tilly's efforts to get the implementation of the Edict postponed as a symptom of approaching senility. Consequently, on his arrival in Vienna, he feels justified in not pressing for this postponement. He carries out the letter, but not the spirit, of his mission, and does his utmost to nullify its effect. His subsequent admission that he acted in this ambiguous fashion and his realization that no sophistry can condone his behavior are indicated by his belated summing-up of the grievous consequences which followed on his sin of omission:

> His Imperial Majesty should have been adjured to refrain from doing violence to the conscience of his subjects, to exercise patience until such time as the Holy Spirit would heal the breach. But patience was not exercised in regard to the errant souls and now this very lack of patience is destroying Christianity. Instead of bridging the gap we have widened it. . . . Holy Church will never again attain unity.[18]

In the case of the Jesuit, the evolution from rabid fanaticism to tolerance is rendered credible. Through this portrait le Fort delicately suggests that if he, and others in similar positions, had been less self-opinionated and arrogant, the course of European history might well have been different.

Pastor Bake, like the Jesuit, is a figure in whom the sack

of Magdeburg effects a radical change of outlook. In character, however, the two men are very different. Pastor Bake is fundamentally a weak man, consumed by uncertainty and doubt and by a lack of confidence in his own judgment. From the outset his weakness is patent. Although convinced in his heart that an alliance with the Swedes is no real answer to Magdeburg's problem, Pastor Bake lacks the moral courage to give voice to this opinion, as to do so would entail defying his immediate superior, Dr. Gilbert, who dictated the line of policy to be adopted in dealing with the parishioners. In Pastor Bake's acceptance of this dictation and in allowing himself to be used as a tool in the hands of others lie his particular guilt and responsibility for the disaster.

It is not without significance that the reader's attention is focused on Pastor Bake in the earlier pages of the narrative and that to him are assigned the final words of the conclusion. Le Fort has selected him as the exponent of one of her most deeply held convictions, namely, the unity which prevails between the various Christian denominations in relation to essential doctrines. As the Pastor stands outside his former cathedral after the sack of the town and hears the victorious Catholics within chanting the Credo with which he too is familiar, he realizes in a flash of illumination that he is separated from his Catholic fellow countrymen by "a mere wall erected by human hands and that this wall had been responsible for reducing to rubble and ashes the town of Magdeburg."[19] So he brings out the bitter tragedy of the Thirty Years' War, which placed Christians who shared basic tenets of belief in opposing camps for the ostensible protection of these very beliefs. From the perspective of the present day, le Fort, through Pastor Bake, brings out the futility of this disastrous episode and emphasizes the responsibility of the various protagonists for it. The story does not, however, end on this note of despair, but on a note of hope for the future: as Pastor Bake looks on the ruined town he sees in it a symbol of the hill of Golgotha where all Christendom is united, and with this vision, with its implicit plea for Christian unity, the narrative ends.

The destruction of Magdeburg is shown as having made it clear to all those concerned that there is no hope for peaceful coexistence with those of different outlook "until *caritas* is restored to its rightful place, for without it the destruction of the world is inevitable."[20] Of the four main characters, Willigis and General Tilly have appreciated this from the outset, but they are unsuccessful in their endeavor to impart to others their own conviction; Pastor Bake has stifled within himself the voice of conscience that told him *caritas* should have governed his dealings even with his enemies, and the Jesuit only learns his mistake as a result of the destruction of Magdeburg. By making these characters vehicles for ideas le Fort has made her major themes explicit; in a similar manner the subsidiary themes of the book reach the reader through Falkenberg, Erdmuth Plögen and Frau Bake.

The Swedish commander Falkenberg is essentially the professional soldier. The ideological issues of the war concern him not at all and he is sublimely untroubled by any conflicting loyalties. To him war has become an end in itself, and in its service he has become a complete fanatic. This automaton-like figure, "serious as death itself and as inflexible as an immutable decree,"[21] seems to move in an orbit remote from ordinary human values, and he regards Magdeburg and its inhabitants as mere pawns in his great game of war. Any urge Falkenberg may have to serve other ideals is sublimated in his fanatical, almost idolatrous, devotion to the king in whose service he is ready to sacrifice his life: "His Majesty will find me ready at all times, either to live or to die as the occasion demands."[22] That these are no idle words is shown by his subsequent death in battle.

It is difficult to overlook the correspondence between Falkenberg and the type of Nazi leader that became so well known in Germany in the 1930's, when this book was written. In his remark to Pastor Bake: "I am the sole arbiter of the consciences of the clergy, and anyone who ventures to dispute this will be hanged,"[23] we have one of the clearest indications of this correspondence. Such an attitude in regard to individual liberty of conscience is one which was commonly evinced during the Nazi regime, and it would seem clear that in her depiction of this character le Fort was very much influenced by the political background of the day. The portrait of Falkenberg may be regarded as a timely warning to her fellow countrymen of the threat to individual liberty which political power may bring in its train and of the danger of exploitation inherent in it. His characteristic features are an undeviating devotion to his ideal and a complete ruthlessness in its pursuit. The soldier Falkenberg—like Enzio in *The Wreath of Angels*—is in effect the quintessence of what Nietzsche designated the "will to power" (*Wille zur Macht*). He is possessed of great force of personality and of an uncommonly high degree of control both over his own will and over the wills of others. In his dealings with Erdmuth and Pastor Bake, characteristic features of the *Machtmensch* are evidenced, above all the contemptuous treatment of the dupes he employs to serve his own ends.

In the figure of Frau Bake, the Pastor's wife, le Fort is concerned to show that simple purity of heart and unquestioning trust in Divine Providence so conspicuously absent in the other characters. The profound, though unintellectual nature of Frau Bake's Christianity is obvious in her every action; in her concern for her family and friends, and in the saving pity she extends to both Erdmuth and to Falkenberg, and, most strikingly of all, in her attitude toward her fellow Christians who are besieging her native city. Frau Bake's daily life is in effect an application of the basic principles of the Christian ethical code. The broader issues of the war do not concern her, and her chief interest lies in human life in its narrower context of her home and family. The weakness of Frau Bake as a fictitious character lies in the fact that she is more or less an embodiment of le Fort's concept of the truly Christian wife and mother as delineated in the pages of her philosophic treatise on woman, *Die Ewige Frau* (The Eternal Woman).[24] For, despite her virtues, the pastor's wife never really comes to life. A note of cloying sentimentality in this portrait tends to alienate the reader's sympathy, and he cannot but be aware of the fact that here the author is more concerned with the presentation of abstract ideas than with the infusion of poetic life into the character. This character, although incorporating some of le Fort's ideals, may be designated one of the least satisfying aspects of the novel.

Just as Willigis is complemented by the Jesuit, so too Frau Bake is complemented by Erdmuth Plögen, whose qualities are the obverse of those of the pastor's wife. Here we see a self-seeking woman, full of an arrogant pride which motivates all her actions. Erdmuth's role in the story is that of the foolish virgin depicted on the walls of the cathedral at Magdeburg. At the beginning of the novel an element of suspense as to her fate is introduced: she is described seated in the cathedral "her countenance somewhat broad and full, but in its own peculiar way attractive and beautiful, like the faces of the wise and foolish virgins depicted on the arch over the Gate of Paradise. Erdmuth actually looked as if she had come down from that arch."[25] But whether her role is to be that of the wise or of the foolish virgin is as yet an open question. From the moment, however, that Erdmuth decides that Willigis has deserted her, she undergoes a change, and it is clear that her role is to be that of the foolish virgin. Blinded by her injured pride, she determines to demonstrate to her little world her self-sufficiency. She retreats into herself and begins to live in a world of fantasy. The relationship between Erdmuth and Falkenberg is part of this fantasy. Between them there is no real love, for each is merely exploiting the other for his own selfish ends. Erdmuth herself willfully refuses to see the true nature of their relationship. The realist Falkenberg sardonically remarks: "She truly thinks that I am going to lead her to the altar, and in reality I am leading her to the grave."[26] The downfall of Magdeburg is the factor which brings Erdmuth into contact with reality once more, but the experience is a bitter one, as she, like the city, falls victim to the conquerors.

The correspondence between the fate of the proud Erdmuth and that of Magdeburg has been carefully worked out by le Fort. As Erdmuth has impatiently refused to await the return of her fiancé, Willigis, and has turned to the false bridegroom, Falkenberg, in his stead, so Magdeburg is unfaithful to its Kaiser and enters into the alliance with the Swedish king. Both break a plighted troth, for as Erdmuth had been espoused to Willigis by her parents in accordance with the custom of the age, Magdeburg was indissolubly bound to the Reich. Erdmuth, like Magdeburg, is used as a pawn in the great game of diplomacy; she believes Falkenberg's promise that King Gustav, her protector, will take up residence under her roof and she awaits his arrival with impatience. As she enjoys the new importance this promise confers on her, so too Magdeburg relaxes, deluded into an illusion of security. Pride, however, is ultimately the cause of the downfall of both Erdmuth and Magdeburg, and they are destined to share in the final humiliation.

The characters of *The Wedding at Magdeburg* fit into a well-defined, discernible structural plan. The argument of the novel is centered on a conflict between two opposing groups, the Protestant citizens of Magdeburg and the Catholic soldiers of the Reich. The individuals within these groups are not characterized in detail, but through them le Fort endeavors to portray the general point of view and the workings of the group mind. Both groups share in broad outline the same characteristics, namely, an inability to see events in a context wider than the purely personal, and a consequent failure to bring a clearheaded approach to bear on the problems confronting them. Le Fort has presented the conflicting Catholic and Protestant groups with impartiality, ignoring all barriers of creed: each group has its progressive and its unenlightened representatives. As we have seen, both Willigis and Tilly represent dissentient voices within their respective groups: both have a more perceptive and penetrating grasp of the situation than their respective coreligionists, as a result of which an acute personal crisis is created for both of them. The role of the shortsighted Pastor Bake is likewise balanced by that of the hotheaded Jesuit. This neat juxtaposition and contrast of the characters—also evident in the case of the minor characters—together with the concern for balance and harmony on the part of the author, gives an overall impression of a disciplined and ordered approach to the material. Most of the characters have a lifelike quality and their individual problems and worries succeed in engaging the reader's sympathy and in retaining his interest. There is, however, little question of psychological motivation of the action, which is carried forward by the tide of outward events. The role played by the various characters is predominantly passive; they talk and engage in long arguments and counter-arguments in reasoning out their positions, but cannot really be said to control events.

The action of the novel, like the characters, adheres to a basic scheme. It develops in three distinct stages, each stage being carefully related to the fate of the city and to that of Erdmuth Plögen. There are no irrelevant digressions, and the action gathers momentum and mounts steadily to the inevitable climax with the minimum of deviation. The impassioned arguments and reasoning introduce an element of tension, but there is little action in the usual sense of the word as applied to an historical novel. Its place is taken largely by argument and ratiocination, such action as there is being for the most part on the mental plane. The language of *The Wedding at Magdeburg* is characterized by a high degree of economy and lucidity. Consequent on the nature of the story, and on le Fort's approach to it, a high proportion of the narrative is cast in the form of dialogue, and the manner in which the dialogue is introduced—very often reminiscent of that used in playwriting—helps to emphasize and bring out its inherently dramatic qualities. The swift thrust and parry of words, the alternating quick and slow movements, the impassioned urgency on one side paralleled by the playing for time on the other, create an element of tension and excitement which is seldom relaxed. The deliberately archaic style of the narrative—le Fort seems to aim at re-echoing the contemporary chronicle style—further helps to bring the reader close to the events and characters depicted; it encourages him to think in their idiom and to see things through their eyes. The few short descriptive passages serve to relieve the tension between the various episodes and, over and above this, have often a symbolic or an elucidatory significance.

The most remarkable single stylistic feature of *The Wedding at Magdeburg* is the use of the allegory. As already indicated, Erdmuth and her relationship to Willigis stand as an allegory for Magdeburg and its relationship to the Reich, and the events which lead to her fate are an accurate parallel to the events preceding the sack of the city. The courtship of Erdmuth and the sack of Magdeburg are described by a common terminology. The city is spoken of repeatedly as a maiden sought in marriage by two rival claimants, and in the toast of the belligerent Pappenheim we have an excellent illustration of the use of these terms of reference:

> That we should all link arms and, forming a circle, dance round the beautiful bride until her breath fails. That we should light the torches for her wedding night. That we should conduct her to her lawful bridal couch as His Imperial Majesty has decreed—to this I raise my glass and drink a toast to her royal bridegroom: I drink to the next victory of our invincible supreme commander Tilly. I drink to the wedding at Magdeburg.[27]

Even the stern and unimaginative Falkenberg unbends so far as to adopt this allegorical terminology:

> His Royal Majesty the King of Sweden offers his hand today to the Magdeburg maiden in token of an alliance, using me as his proxy, as is the custom of noble potentates, praying that this famous wise and noble virgin, who has never yielded to any suitor, may place her wreath in my hands, as the proxy of His Imperial Majesty, promising to love, follow and be faithful to His Majesty in all things.[28]

In order to put forward the paradoxical theme of the novel in such a manner it will be easily understood that le Fort presents the action of this novel in terms of an allegory, and it is for this same reason that she has infused very many of the images she uses with an additional function so that they have become symbols in their own right.

It is convenient to consider the symbols of the novel under two main headings:[29] those which have the function of *directing* the action of the characters and those whose function is merely *illustrative* or elucidatory. Of the first group the most striking is the bullet hole through the heart of the Virgin Mary depicted on Tilly's war-scarred banner, whose significant position is reminiscent of the prophecy of Simeon: "Thine own soul a sword shall pierce." This may be said to determine Tilly's action insofar as it serves to remind him that in matters concerning faith, military victory is no gauge of real success. Another striking example of the symbols which determine the action of the characters is the statue of Kaiser Otto standing on the market place at Magdeburg. This statue serves as a constant reminder to the councillors that their city, by virtue of an old promise of Kaiser Otto, should by right no longer be under Imperial jurisdiction, but should enjoy the privileges of a free city of the Reich. It thus serves to strengthen their resistance to the present Kaiser and encourages them to persist in their recalcitrant attitude.

Both the hole in the banner and the statue of Otto symbolize a concept or an idea; the second group of symbols has a purely illustrative and explanatory function and in this capacity they enrich the narrative. Many of them recur as *leitmotifs*. Foremost among these is the storm which, providing the auditory background for Tilly's council of war, increases and diminishes in intensity with the ebb and flow of human passion, and finally breaks into the council room at the moment when human passions have broken through the restraining bonds of reason. Similarly, the river Elbe with its latent forces stands as a symbol for the citizens of Magdeburg. Although it is quiescent on the surface, its depths are inhabited by "powers and forces of the deep. . . always ready to engulf and submerge man and his work."[30] So too the citizens conceal behind an outwardly calm exterior their resentment of the Kaiser's rash attempt to enforce the Edict, but having once allowed this anger to sway their judgment, they are powerless to arrest the havoc it creates. When their anger subsides it is too late to remedy the situation and they are crushed by the tide of events. Also mentioned repeatedly is the blossoming pear tree, a symbol of the ordered and serene life of the citizens under normal conditions. Just before the storm on the city it is presented in all its glory; "but it was the last glow of its splendour; on the morrow it would be no more."[31]

The quality and effectiveness of symbols in *The Wedding at Magdeburg* vary enormously, some of them, such as the "blossoming pear tree" being highly evocative, others verging on the banal. A few of the symbols (e.g. the hole in the banner) spring from a specifically religious background, and their evocative power is thus limited to the reader familiar with this background. Whereas on the whole they effectively raise the level of the narrative, many of them, by virtue of excessive elaboration, are not wholly effective. Both allegory and symbolism are best perceived imaginatively, and invariably lose in effect through elucidation and elaboration. Le Fort's eagerness to guide the reader to the significance of her symbols often weakens their force and her appeals to our intellectual rather than to our imaginative faculties detract from the evocative potential of the story.

The Wedding at Magdeburg appeared in 1938, when Nazism was at its height in Germany, when political fanaticism and the desire for military supremacy and power were beginning to effect the lives of countless thousands. At this time Christians of all denominations were beginning to become increasingly aware of the necessity for cooperation and for the formation of a bulwark against the encroachments of the common enemy. If we look at the problems raised by the novel against this background it will be clear that they are in no way peculiar to the historical context in which they are here depicted, but that they are of universal significance, and indeed are highly topical. *The Wedding at Magdeburg*, with its clear exposition of the proper relation of Protestant and Catholic to one another and of each group to the ruling authority, represents le Fort's positive contribution to ecumenical thought; it brings the mistakes of history into sharp focus and encourages reflection on issues which are today becoming increasingly vital to Christians all over the world.

CHAPTER IV

1. Die Erkenntnis, dass die Glaubensspaltung in letzter religiöser Schau weniger eine Spaltung des Glaubens ist als eine Spaltung der Liebe, und dass die theologische Überwindung jener niemals gelingen kann, wenn ihr nicht die Überwindung dieser bereits voraufgegangen ist. "Zum 70 Geburtstag von Karl Muth," *Aufzeichnungen*, p. 79.
2. Cf. A. F. Baecker, *The Treatment of History in the Works of Gertrud von le Fort*, dissertation (Cincinnati, 1956).
3. C. V. Wedgwood, *History of The Thirty Years War* (London, 1938), p. 242.
4. Es könne wohl sein, dass dieser Abend noch der Jungfrauenabend der Stadt Magdeburg werde. *Schriften* II, p. 314.
5. Der Schlüssel aller Dinge. *Ibid.*, p. 307.
6. Auf dem Schachbrett zweier feindlicher Armeen, jetzt vollkommen mattgesetzt. *Schriften* II, p. 479.
7. Wenn der Rat zu Magdeburg wirklich kaiserlich sein will, so muss er in kaiserliche Devotion zurückkehren. *Schriften* II, p. 357.
8. Ein prächtiger Mensch, voll guten Willens, allenthaben noch den grossen Ordnungen der Dinge zugewandt. *Ibid.*, p. 365.
9. Wenn Kaiserliche Majestät nicht auf das Edikt verzichtet, dann kann kein Protestant kaiserlich sein. *Ibid.*, p. 358.
10. Es ist nicht möglich, dass Glaube und Reich zweierlei Befehl ausgeben... Glaube kann sich doch nur auf Gott allein verlassen. *Schriften* II, p. 358.
11. Was ein Mensch glaube das ist nicht kaiserlicher Majestät Sache, sondern Gottes Sache. *Ibid.*, p. 481.
12. Die Liebe ist stark wie der Tod. *Schriften* II, p. 294.
13. Im Grunde weiss ich nichts weiter, als dass ich ein Soldat bin: ein Soldat muss der Ratio belli gehorsamen. *Ibid.*, p. 364.
14. Die Exzellenz sah aus, als stehe sie ganz allein irgendwo in einem entblätterten Wald, da fiel gleichsam von allen Seiten her ein herbstliches Licht voll auf sie herab. *Schriften* II, p. 454.
15. Man wird die Exzellenz zum finsteren Fanatiker des Glaubens stempeln, man wird den Ruhm der Katholischen Excellenz an-

tasten. . . die Exzellenz wird für Verbrechen leiden müssen, die sie nicht begangen hat. *Ibid.*, pp. 511, 512.

16. Maria siegte nicht mit dem Schwert in der Hand, Maria siegte mit dem Schwert im Herzen, sie siegte durch die leidende Liebe ihres göttlichen Sohnes. *Schriften* II, p. 364.

17. Mitten in der Niederlage. . . das ist der Sieg. *Ibid.*, p. 512.

18. "Man hätte sie (Kaiserliche Majestät) beschwören müssen, den Gewissen nicht Gewalt anzutun, Geduld zu üben, bis der Geist die Spaltung überwindet! Allein man hat mit den abgefallenen Seelen keine Geduld gehabt. . . und nun geht an der Geduldlosigkeit der Christenheit die Christenheit zugrunde! Statt den Spalt zu schliessen, haben wir ihn tiefer aufgebrochen. . . niemals wird die heilige Kirche wieder einig werden. *Schriften* II, p. 509.

19. Eine einzige Mauer, von Menschenhand errichtet. . . Und um dieser Mauer willen war ganz Magdeburg in Schutt und Asche gesunken! *Schriften* II, p. 519.

20. Bevor nicht die christliche Liebe wiederum in ihre Rechte eingesetzt sei, die Welt ohne diese könne nur zerstören. *Schriften* II, p. 517.

21. Ernst wie der Tod und entschlossen wie ein unentrinnbarer Befehl. *Schriften* II, p. 335.

22. Mich soll Königliche Majestät allezeit bereit finden, zu leben oder zu sterben, wie die Sache es verlangt. *Ibid.*, p. 421.

23. Das Gewissen der Herren Pastoren bestimme jetzt ich, und jeden, der das zu bestreiten wagt, werde ich hängen lassen. *Ibid.*, p. 436.

24. *Die Ewige Frau* (Kösel, 1934).

25. Das Gesicht etwas breit und voll, aber doch auf seine besondere Weise schön und lieblich wie die Gesichter der klugen und der törichten Jungfrauen draussen im Gewände der Paradiesespforte —ja geradezu wie stracks von dort heruntergestiegen sah die Jungfer Erdmuth aus. *Schriften* II, p. 291.

26. Sie denkt wahrhaftig, ich werde sie zum Altar führen, und ich führe sie zum Grab. *Schriften* II, p. 415.

27. Das wir allesamt einen Kreis um die schöne Braut schliessen und mit ihr tanzen dürfen, bis ihr der Atem ausgeht! Dass wir ihr die Fackeln anzünden dürfen zur Hochzeitsnacht! Dass wir sie ins rechte Brautbett legen dürfen, wie es ihr Kaiserliche Majestät bestimmt hat—darauf erhebe ich mein Glas und trinke ihrem Herrn Bräutigam zu: ich trinke auf die nächste Victorie unseres unbesieglichen Generalissimus Tilly. Ich trinke auf die Magdeburgische Hochzeit. *Schriften* II, p. 381.

28. So haben sich Königliche Majestät von Schweden die Sprache dieser hochberühmten Stadt Magdeburg zu eigen gemacht und lassen dieselbe wissen, dass sie am heutigen Tage, wie erlauchte Potentaten pflegen, durch Prokuration der Magdeburgischen Jungfrau die Hand zum Bunde reichen. Also möge nun diese hochberühmte, kluge und herrliche Jungfrau, deren Stolz sich noch keinem ihrer Freier ergeben hat, ihren Kranz vertrauensvoll in die Hände des hier anwesenden Prokurators Königlicher Majestät legen, demselben hinfort Treue, Gefolgschaft und Gehorsam leistend in allen Stücken. *Schriften* II, p. 395.

29. This classification of symbols has been used by J. van der Ligt in his detailed analysis of le Fort's use of symbolism in *Die Symbolik in den Romanen der Gertrud von le Fort* (Breukelen, 1958).

30. Die Mächte und Gewalten der Tiefe. . . allezeit bereit, ihn und sein Werk zu verschlingen. *Schriften* II, p. 340.

31. Aber es war die letzte Pracht, morgen würde sie fallen. *Schriften* II, p. 444.

CHAPTER V

Gate of Heaven

Gate of Heaven (1954) ranks among the best short stories written by le Fort in postwar years. A comparison of this story with her earlier works will show that a development has taken place in her literary technique and that her philosophic thought has come to cover a wider field than previously. In the works already discussed conflict between characters of different confessions and beliefs supplies the basis of the argument: in *The Veil of Veronica* the conflict is between paganism and Christianity, in *The Song at the Scaffold* it is between the mystical and the practical approach to the supernatural, and in *The Wedding at Magdeburg*, confessional differences between Catholics and Protestants form a vital part of the plot. In *Gate of Heaven* the perspective has widened and the central issue has broadened: this novelle deals with the relationship between faith and science, and is concerned with the possibility of the survival of the central truth of Christianity in a scientific age.

Gate of Heaven, like *The Song at the Scaffold*, is a novelle in which le Fort has employed the framework technique to good effect. There is, however, a difference in her use of this technique in the two works: in *The Song at the Scaffold* the framework is a letter, written contemporaneously with the events of the story proper; in *Gate of Heaven* le Fort has varied her use of the device. Here the central episode, which takes place in Italy in the early seventeenth century, is given added significance and depth by being set off against a framework set in twentieth-century Germany. This particular period has been selected by le Fort for the framework in order to highlight some of the differences and analogies between the two ages and so to throw light on her main theme from two perspectives simultaneously.

The "Galilean document," an account of events connected with the trial of Galileo written by one of his students, is the center point of *Gate of Heaven*. It deals with events which took place in a period vibrant with radical questions and doubts. Galileo's discovery that the sun, and not the earth, was the axis around which the planets revolve was calculated to upset completely the medieval concept of the importance of man's place in the universe and his pre-eminent position in the scheme of things. The earth was now revealed as an insignificant subsidiary planet, and to many it seemed that a revision of human values and a new approach to the question of human destiny must be undertaken. The sudden impact of this reversal of values brought enormous difficulties in its train for the contemporary Church. Hitherto "the sun stood still, the moon stayed" had been literally interpreted and had determined cosmic notions. Seventeenth-century theology, with its literal interpretation of Scripture, was now confronted with a scientific discovery in apparent conflict with biblical texts. The ecclesiastical authorities naturally regarded with suspicion any scientific discovery which seemed at variance with the traditional interpretation of the Bible, and were prepared to take immediate steps to silence anyone who questioned their authority. In their zeal for the defence of their faith they made the mistake of dogmatizing on matters of science and of demanding that their teachings on these matters be regarded as *de fide*. Such is the background against which the Galilean story before us is played out. A brief discussion of the reactions of its four main characters to the new picture of the cosmos and to the resultant problems will indicate the nature of the questions le Fort wishes to pose in this story, as well as the solutions she suggests as being relevant to our own times.

The problem on which the "Galilean document" centers is stated simply and dispassionately at the outset of the story. "The earth was no longer the center of the universe, it was just a simple tiny planet circling humbly with its one moon around the sun."[2] The reader is introduced to various members of the Catholic intelligentsia and ecclesiastical circles in Rome, and their individual reactions to this opening statement are presented. These reactions vary in accordance with the basic attitudes of their holders and also with their respective degrees of scientific knowledge. The fact that apart from Diana, niece of the Cardinal and an ardent admirer of Galileo, none of the main characters is assigned a Christian name stresses the representative nature of his role. Galileo's name is never specifically mentioned: he is the Master—the moving spirit in the vanguard of scientific research; the Cardinal is primarily a typical ecclesiastic of his day, and the young German, author of the document, is described as the Student, a disciple of the new science. Each of these figures represents a different viewpoint and here, as in le Fort's other works, it is through their involvement in one another and in the central issue of the story that its problems are made explicit.

Diana is a somewhat insubstantial and vaguely delineated figure who scarcely comes to life as a personality. Her reaction to the situation in which she finds herself is typical of that of many of her contemporaries, and it is as representative of a group attitude that her dilemma is of interest. Now that the earth has shrunk to such diminutive proportions Diana no longer finds herself able to subscribe to the doctrine of the redemption of mankind by the Son of God; she finds herself incapable of adjusting her earlier faith to the new aspect of the universe. Failing to see what relevance Christianity can have to the new picture of the cosmos, she is utterly bewildered, and strives to replace her lost faith in Christ by a new humanitarianism: "We have no longer got a God Who is concerned with us, we have only got ourselves. . . From now on man must be all-in-all to man."[3] Her optimistic trust in human solidarity and the inherent goodness of human nature, however, founders in the hour of trial; neither her uncle, the Cardinal, nor Galileo, whom she loves, evinces innate nobility when put to the test, but rather a pitiable weakness. Diana's ultimate fate is not recounted, but we leave her spiritually bankrupt by the collapse of those values in which she had placed her confidence and trust.

Whereas from the outset Diana has eyes only for the irreconcilable cleavage between traditional faith and science, the Student conscientiously strives to reconcile one with the other. This attempt, however, proves ultimately unavailing, and the reader may follow clearly his evolution from belief to agnosticism. The Student's initial attitude is "that one may accept the new picture of the universe and yet remain a Christian."[4] He stresses the point that Galileo himself never intimated that his discoveries might be incompatible with Christianity. At this stage the Student's faith is still strong enough to permit the assertion: "I know that God exists and will live on as the Lord of creation, regardless of my understanding or ignorance of the laws of nature."[5] The first weakening of his optimistic hope that the two realms of truth, religious and scientific, might coexist in harmony is caused by the rigid attitude of the contemporary churchmen, an attitude reflected in the self-righteous words of one of the cler-

ics: "Holy Church decides what is truth."[6] As events gradually begin to undermine the Student's trust in the integrity
and probity of his fellowmen, he comes to realize that a conflict is inevitable. The course of events at the trial marks the
final stage of the metamorphosis in his attitude. In the Student's eyes both the Cardinal by his condemnation and Gal-
lileo by his recantation are guilty of a betrayal of truth. Their
craven behavior, he feels, justifies his decision to place his
trust henceforth in neither God nor man, but to dedicate
his life from now on to the defence of what he terms "truth
so basely betrayed."[7] He leaves Rome, a bitterly disappointed
and disillusioned man: "I became a new individual for whom
there were no restrictions, for whom the only binding law
would be that of independent research."[8] The short-sighted-
ness of the ecclesiastical authorities, together with their arrogant attitude, has resulted in the loss of an immortal soul;
the cleavage between faith and science is complete for the
Student, the door to a reconciliation between them is irrev-
ocably closed.

Perhaps the most interesting character of the story is Diana's uncle, the Cardinal, who stands as a representative of
the contemporary Church. As he is both a man of science
and a churchman the carefully drawn figure of the Cardinal
incorporates in his person the basic problem of the story.
As a scientist the Cardinal appears to accept as valid Galileo's
daring hypotheses, but this acceptance places him in a dilemma as a churchman. While he admits that Galileo's theories
may in themselves be incontrovertible, he sees that from the
point of view of the Church they may nonetheless present
dangerous pitfalls to the majority of believers. For a short
time the attitude of the Cardinal remains fluid, but gradually
his trust in the ordinary man's ability to accept the new discoveries without danger to his faith gives way to his fears
that man will be unable to find a place for God in the new

cosmos. His attitude hardens and crystallizes when he sees his worst fears confirmed by the defection of his beloved niece, Diana. Her abandonment of the world of belief to which his own life is dedicated and her inability to integrate the new discoveries with her traditional faith ultimately determine the course of action he pursues. From her weakness he deduces the weakness of mankind in general: "My niece is not and never will be intellectually able to cope with the new cosmos, for man as such cannot cope with it."[9] Consequent on this conviction the Cardinal sees it as his duty to condemn Galileo's teaching publicly, even though he is intellectually convinced of the validity of his scientific discoveries.

Le Fort introduces some attenuating circumstances in an attempt to explain, if not to justify, the part the Cardinal plays in the condemnation of Galileo. He is portrayed as a man of blameless life, who remains aloof from the voluptuous pleasures of the contemporary Roman scene, ascetic in his tastes, dedicated to learning and the duties of his high office. This office, however, carries with it great responsibility, and the Cardinal, by virtue of his exalted position, is a man pulled by conflicting forces; he is placed in circumstances which would seem to demand the sacrifice of his intellectual convictions in the interest of expediency. As a priest he is convinced that there can be no conflict between scientific truth and revealed religion, yet he has not the courage necessary to face the corollary from this premise, and he refuses to answer the question put to him by the Student: "Could you possibly conceive, or even endure, the thought that our faith is being saved at the cost of an obvious untruth?"[10] In his heart the Cardinal realizes that the condemnation of Galileo, together with the suppression of his discoveries, is not a real solution, but merely the postponement of a final coming-to-terms with the issues involved. Le Fort suggests that this prince of the Church has one inherent weakness of character, namely, lack of trust in Divine Providence. He has no constructive response to the appeal: "Would Your Eminence not consider the possibility that we should leave to God the future destiny of our religion?";[11] he is totally unable to envisage what form such a "leaving to Divine Providence" should take. His vision of future ages is dominated by the idea that "mankind will ultimately bring about the destruction of the world,"[12] for he is convinced that "the price of knowledge is always death."[13] The Cardinal cannot muster sufficient trust in God to leave the outcome of the inevitable clash in His hands and, weakly following the line of least resistance, takes the necessary steps to enforce the suppression of Galileo's discoveries. Through the weakness of the Cardinal le Fort indicates the point wherein lay the tragic guilt of the Church he represents. Had he but had faith and trust in God's ability to uphold the majesty and power of truth, the course of the relationship between the Church and science might well have been different.

The climax of the story is the scene of the trial of Galileo by the ecclesiastical court. History presents Galileo in the final scenes of his trial as a man broken by fear of death, repudiating a scientific truth of which he is intellectually convinced, and tradition would have us believe that a moment after his recantation he was heard to mutter the words *"Eppur si muove"* (But it did move). Such a figure may inspire pity and compassion, but le Fort presents Galileo in a very different light. Her Galileo is not merely convinced that his scientific deductions are correct, but he also realizes that the more intelligent of his judges share his views. He therefore decides to outdo them in a betrayal of truth, and in ringing, almost jubilant, tones he makes the required recantation, his whole bearing expressive of his contempt both for himself and for his inquisitors. As he speaks, his hearers realize that his words of recantation are but an empty formula, completely at variance with his real convictions. In uttering them he tramples underfoot the last vestiges of his honor and his self-respect: the spectators see "a man trample on his own personality as if it were just a fragment of indifferent matter."[14] But as Galileo's personal moral stature diminishes, the power and majesty of truth seem to grow and fill that silent courtroom: all present realize that truth will ultimately prevail, that the scene being enacted before them is but a travesty of justice and that the condemnation of his teaching will prove ineffective in calling a halt to the progress of science. Galileo's thoughts are an expression of the unvoiced fears of many of those present: "The science I represent is something great and glorious. Whether you condemn it or I retract is equally unimportant. This science is something inviolable which will brook no restraint. . . My teaching will prevail in the future."[15] The concluding stages of the trial are highlighted by an effective use of symbolism. As Galileo is led away, the lights on the table in the courtroom slowly flicker and die, the resultant darkness prefiguring the temporary extinction of the light of knowledge and truth and the victory of pusillanimity and ignorance. The door that closes behind the departing figure of the Master with chilling finality symbolizes the barrier that will exist between the Church and the spirit of free investigation down through the ages as a result of the events just enacted.

This original and sensitive approach by a twentieth-century writer to events which overshadowed Italian history at the beginning of the seventeenth century makes *Gate of Heaven* one of le Fort's best short stories. Her poetic genius and her sense of history have enabled her to project herself into the temper of that age, and she characteristically rejects the popular facile explanation of the condemnation of Galileo. To assume, as is so frequently done, that his judges were reactionaries and obscurantists is, for le Fort, too facile and superficial a solution. Her imaginative intuitive gifts enable her to appreciate and to present sympathetically the dilemma of the members of the ecclesiastical court. She makes it clear that these churchmen, of whom the Cardinal is typical, regarded it as their primary duty to preserve intact the deposit of faith and to transmit unaltered to posterity the fundamental truths of the Old and New Testaments. Their office was primarily the cure of souls, and their duty to preserve from all danger of heresy the flock entrusted to their pastoral care. They were convinced that if the new scientific truths were allowed to percolate among the unlettered, these truths would undermine the simple faith of the people. According to the dictates of human prudence, therefore, these theories must be suppressed until the minds of the faithful would be conditioned gradually to their acceptance by the spread of education and knowledge. Le Fort stresses the worldly wisdom of this approach, but condemns it as unworthy of the high office of the churchmen. Their training in philosophy and theology should have made them realize that one truth cannot possibly be at variance with another; if their faith had been strong, they would have left the solution of a problem that seemed humanly insoluble to the Source of all knowledge. Evasion and postponement were acts of weakness, for which their successors have had to pay the penalty.

Le Fort's deep appreciation of the issues involved in the trial of Galileo and, more particularly, of their relevance to the modern world, is thrown into strong relief in the framework within which the story is set. Here she views the problems dispassionately from the vantage-point of the twentieth century. The prodigious advances of modern science and the conquest of space pose for her and for her Christian contemporaries problems as fundamental and far-reaching as any confronting the Church in the time of Galileo. In her view the Christian today, warned by the example of the past, has a duty not to shirk the problems and issues with which modern scientific advances confront him, but he should have the courage to grapple with them and reconcile them with his basic tenets and his ethical code. She effectively correlates the problems of the seventeenth century with those of today by setting the "Galilean document" within a framework of Germany during the course of World War II, where its theme is re-echoed in a modern context against a background of indiscriminate bombing and total warfare. The characters who figure in the framework are confronted with what is fundamentally the same basic problem as confronted Diana and the Student. Today we would seem to have reached the ultimate limit of the divorce of science from faith which started with Galileo. In face of such episodes as the destruction of Hiroshima or of Dresden, where man's inhumanity to man has transcended all previous experience, the fear voiced by the Cardinal that "once the belief in God has ceased to exist the world will recognize no restraining influence"[16] has become a reality, and his vision of the man of future ages fated to live in a universe without a God has been realized.

The young Doctor of science who figures in the framework is, in many respects, the intellectual heir to Diana's ideas, and the divorce of science from faith which we saw beginning with Diana has become absolute for him. Many of the anomalies of the modern man of science are incorporated in this young Doctor. His highly advanced technical knowledge is not balanced by a correspondingly high degree of spiritual maturity and, although he is apparently satisfied with his autonomous position, he still has an uneasy fear that one day he may discover a transcendental truth which will prevail, a fear that he may yet find himself face to face with a God Whom he could acknowledge and Whose laws might interfere with or limit the scope of his scientific advances. The wheel, however, has not as yet come full circle, and the Doctor intends in the meantime to exploit his spiritual and intellectual independence to the best advantage. Modern scientific developments have proved to be an accurate realization of Galileo's forecast. By bringing out the contrast between the position of Galileo and that of the Doctor, le Fort makes explicit the important change that has taken place in man's relation to these developments: in the seventeenth century man believed himself master of natural forces; today he is in danger of becoming their slave, and of losing his power to direct their progress. He has liberated a force which is proving stronger than its master.

In this story le Fort has used the structural framework to add another dimension to her basic theme and, by juxtaposing the seventeenth-century predicament with that of our own times, she has succeeded in effecting a counterbalance between the respective similarities and differences between the two periods. Be the setting medieval or modern, the nature of the basic human predicament remains unchanged; it is the task of each individual to work out a solution in harmony with his particular circumstances and times. The story is written in a clear and straightforward manner. No unnecessary detail is introduced; the background is lightly sketched and the characters are immediately engaged in the action. Although it is true that they seem to have interested le Fort less as persons than as representatives of particular ideas and points of view, they nonetheless arouse the sympathy and involvement of the reader, and the interaction of these characters, together with the clash of their opposing views, imparts to the story an element of dramatic tension which is skillfully sustained throughout. By virtue of the clarity and skill with which the story is presented and, above all, of the relevance of its problems to the present day, *Gate of Heaven* remains one of the most popular and topical of le Fort's short stories.

CHAPTER V

1. English translation, *Gate of Heaven* (Chicago: Henry Regnery, 1962).
2. Die Erde... befand sich nicht im Mittelpunkt der Welt, sie war ein kleiner einfacher Planet, der mit seinem einem Mond demütig um die Sonne kreiste. *Schriften* III, p. 469.
3. Wir haben keinen Gott mehr, der sich um uns kümmert, wir haben nur noch uns selbst! Hinfort muss der Mensch dem Menschen alles sein. *Schriften* III, p. 471.
4. Dass man die neue Wissenschaft bekennen und gleichwohl ein Christ sein kann. *Ibid.*
5. Ich weiss, dass Gott der Herr der Schöpfung ist und bleibt, gleichviel was ich von ihr erkenne oder nicht erkenne. *Ibid.*, p. 485.
6. Was Wahrheit ist, stellt die Heilige Kirche fest. *Ibid.*, p. 485.
7. Die verstossene Wahrheit, *Schriften* III, p. 509.
8. Ein neuer Mensch (stieg) in mir auf, für den es keine Bindungen mehr gab, sondern nur noch das Gesetz der freien Forschung. *Ibid.*, p. 512.
9. Meine Nichte ist dem neuen Weltbild nicht gewachsen, sie wird es niemals sein, denn der Mensch als solcher ist ihm nicht gewachsen. *Schriften* III, pp. 491, 492.
10. Können Sie sich denken, nein, Können Sie den Gedanken ertragen, dass der Glaube durch eine offene Unwahrheit gerettet wird? *Schriften* III, p. 501.
11. Halten Sie es nicht für möglich, Eminenz, dass man die Geschicke des Glaubens ganz einfach Gott anheim geben sollte? *Ibid.*, p. 501.
12. Die Menschheit einst den Untergang der Welt heraufbeschwören wird. *Ibid.*, p. 499.
13. Die Erkenntnis wird stets mit dem Tode bezahlt. *Ibid.*, p. 499.
14. Einen Menschen über seine eigene Person hinwegschreiten wie über ein Stück gleichgültiger Materie. *Schriften* III, p. 507.
15. Meine Wissenschaft ist gross und herrlich! Ob ihr sie verurteilt und ob ich sie widerrufe, das ist eins so gleichgültig wie das andere—diese Wissenschaft ist unantastbar und unaufhaltsam... Meine Wissenschaft wird Siegerin der Zukunft sein. *Ibid.*, pp. 507, 508.
16. Wenn der Glaube an Gott erloschen ist, wird sich die Welt vor nichts mehr fürchten. *Schriften* III, p. 491.

Conclusion

Since this *Introduction* does not attempt to present the reader with more than a representative selection of le Fort's fiction, the concluding comments will be confined to the works we have discussed—always bearing in mind that these are fairly characteristic both of her thought and of her manner of expression. In the Introduction we suggested that le Fort is one of the few engaged writers in Germany today who has successfully combined a deep personal commitment with a high degree of literary skill and that she seems to be chiefly important as an exponent of ideas; let us now draw together the thematic threads which run through the works we have discussed.

Le Fort's basic theme is the question of man's relationship to God. She has viewed this problem in a variety of settings and against many different historical backgrounds, yet in each work the central issue is fundamentally the same: no matter in what period or environment man is placed, he must cope with and work out for himself what for le Fort is the crucial problem of all existence—his position *vis-à-vis* his Creator. The second theme fundamental to her prose work is that of human relationships. On a very broad basis this theme might be said to be that of almost any novelist, but under the pen of le Fort it has taken on a new significance. As we have indicated, all le Fort's work is conditioned by her background and by her ideological commitment. She accordingly approaches the theme of human relationships from an unusual angle and views it in the context of the *corpus Christi mysticum*. As members of this mystical body all men are intimately bound together: no man is an island and each must bear a measure of responsibility for others. Thus le Fort never views human actions in isolation, but is constantly concerned to communicate her own acute consciousness of their endless repercussions. It is for this reason that many of her characters find fulfillment by sacrificing themselves and their interests for others—one thinks immediately of Veronica in *The Wreath of Angels* and of Blanche de la Force—and that such stress is laid on the value of vicarious suffering. The third basic theme is a natural corollary from le Fort's religious standpoint and is closely connected with the two themes mentioned above; we refer to the theme of the impact of divine grace on human life. Le Fort is continually concerned to demonstrate the relevance of the supernatural to human existence and, since she views grace as the main channel through which God directly intervenes in men's lives, it often plays an important role in her fiction. As a result of the impact of grace the normal human values frequently suffer a reversal in her work; while from a purely rational point of view the lives of characters like Blanche or General Tilly may not be judged to have been particularly successful, le Fort has indicated in each case that on a deeper spiritual level the purpose of their individual lives has been fulfilled.

No survey, however brief, of le Fort's work would be complete without mention of her concept of the role of woman. Although this is not exactly a major theme of her writing, it is fundamental to her thought[1] and has influenced her in all her portraits of female characters. Le Fort is by no means a femininist or an advocate of woman's playing an important role in public affairs; on the contrary, she sees woman essentially as the giver and protector of life, dedicated to the welfare of mankind, but by preference striving after perfection in the seclusion of her home. Woman's life is to le Fort essentially one of self-effacement and humility in the service of others. Her special prerogative is *giving*— we have noted that her heroines Blanche and Veronica are both characterized by their readiness to *give* and to forego personal happiness in the interests of others. In the figures of Frau Seide in *The Wreath of Angels* and of Erdmuth in *The Wedding at Magdeburg* the negative side of the picture is presented: when woman betrays her true nature and refuses to *give*, disaster will inevitably follow sooner or later;[2] neither Seide nor Erdmuth achieves even a modicum of happiness for herself or for others.

Many other themes occur with greater or lesser degrees of frequency in le Fort's writings; we will mention only two of these which have a particular relevance to the present-day situation, namely, the question of Christian unity and that of the difficulties presented by the advancement of science. The sad cleavage within the ranks of Christendom is a problem of which le Fort is painfully aware, and an excellent illustration of her clear and positive thought on this problem— which has also figured prominently in her recent writing— is afforded by *The Wedding at Magdeburg*. The problems confronting the Christian in the modern world in the light of modern scientific and technological advances are not easy of solution. Through her fiction, in particular *Gate of Heaven*, le Fort insists that we must come to terms with these problems in the light of our Christian philosophy and that cowardly evasion of the issues with which they confront us will, in the last analysis, prove to be disastrous.

It will be evident that consistency of outlook and uniformity of theme characterize le Fort's work. Such a concentration on a limited number and variety of themes as is evident in her writing could easily have led to a monotonous series of repetitions, but in le Fort's case this danger has been forestalled by a number of factors, above all by the variety of approach to her themes. She continually alters her perspective and throws light on her themes from different angles by setting them against different historical backgrounds. We have seen that although historical backcloth in each case has been of less intrinsic concern to her than the problems she deploys against it, she is nonetheless successful in evoking the atmosphere of the period in which her plots are set and in sustaining a high degree of historical accuracy. Her study of history at Heidelberg under Schubart has clearly deepened her understanding of historical situations and has helped her to select with such a keen and unerring eye accurate historical parallels for contemporary issues and problems. *The Song at the Scaffold, The Wedding at Magdeburg* and *Gate of Heaven*—stories all very different in character, yet all informed by le Fort's characteristic optimistic approach to human life and affairs—bear testimony to her perceptive and original handling of historical situations.

The picture presented by the five works we have discussed of le Fort's development as a prose writer during the period they cover (1928-1954) will have shown that whereas there has been little fluctuation in her ideological approach, a definite evolution and progress in her literary technique may be observed. When talking of le Fort's literary technique, her novels and her novellen, or shorter stories, may be divided into two distinct categories; the same generalizations do not hold good for both genres. In the novels le Fort's weakness as an imaginative creative writer are far

more apparent than in the novellen. In none of her novels
does she employ a formal division into chapters and, in consequence, they suffer from a greater or lesser degree of diffuseness, from a lack of logical development of both plot
and action. The absence of a formal basic structure leads her
to indulge in digressions; discussions and arguments, interesting in themselves, but of little immediate relevance to the
plot, often slow up the development of the action.

The foregoing generalizations do not hold good for le
Fort's novellen. The conventional framework of the novelle
with its disciplined, formal structure counteracts her tendency to diffuseness and digression and throws her many
outstanding gifts into strong relief. Thus within the framework of the novelle those features which prevented her from
achieving complete success with the more flexible form of
the novel tend to disappear: almost without exception, the
novellen are characterized by clarity and lucidity in the treatment of theme, by sharpness in the delineation of character,
speedy engagement of the action and a satisfactory working-
out of the conclusion. Whereas in the novels an element of
tension is rarely to be found, the shorter works are often
built around an incident which contains within itself such
an element; the reader's attention is immediately engaged
and is effortlessly sustained throughout.

Common to both the novels and the novellen is the method
by means of which le Fort presents her main themes. She
invariably puts forward her ideas through the medium of the
characters: each character represents a different attitude to
the central problem, which is viewed simultaneously from
a variety of perspectives. It is then developed in conjunction
with the development of the characters and the action. On
the whole, we may remark, the characters seem to have interested their creator less as individuals in their own right than

as representatives of ideas and ideologies. More emphasis is laid on the clash of ideas and ideals than on that of personalities, and many of these characters accordingly lack the *élan vital* of the successful literary creation. The juxtaposition of divergent views occasionally appears as somewhat contrived and artificial in the earlier novels, but as le Fort gained experience in literary techniques she overcame many of the defects which weaken the force of such works as *The Roman Fountain*. One of the chief merits of her habitual technique just outlined is the involvement of the reader in the issues of the various stories—and this, after all, is le Fort's main purpose in writing. Her method of presenting many possible solutions to the problems she deploys and yet refraining from offering any one of them as decisive encourages thought and participation on the part of the reader and, in the face of the stimulating nature of the topics and of her individualistic approach to them, passive receptivity is virtually impossible. The apparent simplicity of le Fort's work proves to be somewhat deceptive on analysis, and herein lies further testimony to her artistic skill.

The predominant impression conveyed by a study of le Fort's work is that of a pervading unity of thought and theme and of a consistency in outlook. Her concentration on a limited number of themes increases the overall effect of strength and vigor which the work imparts. It is true that Catholic thought frequently supplies the source of her inspiration, yet her work embraces wider horizons. Her art lies in her ability to view human life and endeavor with understanding compassion and to raise her theme above its immediate context to a level where it has a universal significance. At its best, her presentation of theme is powerful, urgent and assured, and in these qualities lie her great strength and her importance as a literary figure.

Gertrud von le Fort

Conclusion

1. In le Fort's short treatise on woman and her role in the world, *Die Ewige Frau* (Kösel, 1934), her views are fully developed.
2. In an interview with the author le Fort indicated that she ascribes many of the ills which have beset her country in recent years to woman's failure to play her appointed role in the scheme of things and to her attempt to arrogate to herself many of the rightful prerogatives of man.

Select Bibliography of Studies
on Gertrud von le Fort

Brugisser, H. *Gertrud von le Fort*. Winterthur, 1959.

Eschbach, M. *Die Bedeutung Gertrud von le Forts in unserer Zeit*. Warendorf, 1948.

Faesi, R. "Gertrud von le Fort," *Christliche Dichter der Gegenwart*, ed. by Friedmann and Mann. Heidelberg, 1955. Pp. 267-83.

Focke, A. *Gertrud von le Fort, Gesamtschau und Grundlagen ihrer Dichtung*. Verlag Styria, 1960.

Kampmann, T. *Gertrud von le Fort, Die Welt einer Dichterin*. Warendorf, Westfalan, 1948.

Grenzmann, W. "Gertrud von le Fort," *Dichtung und Glaube*. Bonn, 1950. Pp. 263-89.

Groensmit, K. H. *Gertrud von le Fort*. Nijmegen, 1950.

Heinen, N. *Gertrud von le Fort*. Luxemburg, 1955.

Jappe, H. *Gertrud von le Fort*. Merano, 1950.

Neuschaffer, W. "The World of Gertrud von le Fort," *German Life and Letters*, 1954-55, p. 30.

Van der Ligt, J. *Die Symbolik in den Romanen der Gertrud von le Fort*. Breukelen, 1958.

Wunderlich, E. M. "Gertrud von le Fort," *The Germanic Review*, 1952. Vol. 27, no. 4, p. 298.